The Homebrewed Christianity
Guide to God

The Homebrewed Christianity Guide to God

Everything You Ever Wanted to Know about the Almighty

ERIC E. HALL
AUTHOR

TRIPP FULLER
SERIES EDITOR

Fortress Press
Minneapolis

THE HOMEBREWED CHRISTIANITY GUIDE TO GOD
Everything You Ever Wanted to Know about the Almighty

Copyright © 2016 Fortress Press. All rights reserved. Except for brief quotations in critical articles or reviews, no part of this book may be reproduced in any manner without prior written permission from the publisher.
Visit http://www.augsburgfortress.org/copyrights/ or write to Permissions, Augsburg Fortress, Box 1209, Minneapolis, MN 55440.

Cover design: Jesse Turri
Book design: PerfecType, Nashville, TN

Library of Congress Cataloging-in-Publication Data
Print ISBN: 978-1-5064-0572-8
eBook ISBN: 978-1-5064-0573-5

The paper used in this publication meets the minimum requirements of American National Standard for Information Sciences — Permanence of Paper for Printed Library Materials, ANSI Z329.48-1984.

Manufactured in the U.S.A.

Contents

Series Introduction

You are about to read a guidebook. Not only is the book the sweet "guide book" size, shaped perfectly to take a ride in your back pocket, but the book itself was crafted with care by a real-deal theology nerd. Here's the thing. The Homebrewed Christianity Guide series has one real goal: we want to think *with* you, not *for* you.

The whole "homebrew" metaphor grows from my passion for helping anyone who wants to geek out about theology to do so with the best ingredients around. That's why I started the Homebrewed Christianity podcast in 2008, and that's why I am thrilled to partner with Fortress Press's Theology for the People team to produce this series. I am confident that the church has plenty of intelligent and passionate people who want a more robust conversation about their faith.

A podcast, in case you're wondering, is like talk radio on demand without the commercials. You download a file and listen when, if, where, and how long you want. I love the podcast medium. Short of talking one-on-one, there's hardly a more intimate presence than speaking to someone in their earbuds as they're stuck in traffic, on the treadmill, or washing dishes. When I started the podcast,

I wanted to give anyone the option of listening to some of the best thinkers from the church and the academy.

Originally, the podcast was for friends, family, and my local pub theology group. I figured people in the group were more likely to listen to a podcast than read a giant book. So as the resident theology nerd, I read the books and then interviewed the authors. Soon, thousands of people were listening. Since then the audience has grown to over fifty thousand unique listeners each month and over a million downloads. A community of listeners, whom we call Deacons, grew, and we've got a cast of co-hosts and regular guests.

Over the better part of a decade, I have talked to scores of theologians and engaged with the Deacons about these conversations. It has been a real joy. Every time I hear from a listener, I do the happy dance in my soul.

And here's the deal: I love theology, but I love the church more. I am convinced that the church can really make a difference in the world. But in order to do that, it needs to face reality rather than run from it. The church must use its brain, live its faith, and join God in working for the salvation of the world. And that's what these books are all about.

We often open and close the podcast by reminding listeners that we are providing the ingredients so that they can brew their own faith. That's the same with these books. Each author is an expert theological brewer, and they've been asked to write from their own point of view. These guidebooks are not boringly neutral; instead, they are zestily provocative, meant to get you thinking and brewing.

I look forward to hearing from you on the Speakpipe at HomebrewedChristianity.com and meeting you at an HBC 3D event. We can drink a pint and talk about this book, how you agree and disagree with it. Because if we're talking about theology, the world is a better place.

And remember: Share the Brew!

Tripp Fuller

The Homebrewed Posse

W hether it's the podcast, the blog, or live events, Homebrewed Christianity has always been a conversation, and these books are no different. So inside of this and every volume in the HBC book, you'll be hearing from four members of the Homebrewed community. They are:

THE BISHOP

The Bishop: Kindly, pastoral, encouraging. She's been around the block a few times, and nothing ruffles her feathers. She wants everyone to succeed, and she's an optimist, so she knows they will.

THE ELDER

The Elder: Scolding, arrogant, know-it-all. He's old and disgruntled, the father figure you can never please. He loves quoting doctrine; he's the kind of guy who controls every church meeting because he knows Roberts Rules of Order better than anyone else.

THE DEACON

The Deacon: Earnest, excited, energetic. He's a guy who has just discovered HBC, and he can't get enough of it. He's a cheerleader, a shouter, an encourager. He's still in his first naïveté.

THE ACOLYTE

The Acolyte: Smart, inquisitive, skeptical. She's the smartest student in your confirmation class. She's bound to be a biologist or a physicist, and she's skeptical of all the hocus pocus of Christianity. But she hasn't given up on it yet, so her questions come from the heart. She really wants to know if all this stuff works.

We look forward to continuing the conversation with you, online and in-person!

Godless in Seattle

I recently became Catholic. To be exact, I became Catholic during the Easter Vigil of 2015 when both my wife and I were confirmed together. The experience was a wonderful one. We have a magnificent cathedral in our little city, one that has no business existing in small-town America. It's too beautiful, and it couldn't have been built except through the gold-monies that funded it a century ago during the Montana gold rush. We also have an outstanding bishop who, in the spirit of Pope Francis, engages his people pastorally, flexibly, lovingly, and in truth. To have received the holy chrism in this setting from a bishop and his right-hand monsignor, both of whom we greatly respect, and from our friend, the campus priest, was a blessing both my wife and I will remember for the rest of our lives. Heck, Grandma ("Maw," as our daughter calls her) even took care of the little one for the evening so that we could actually attend Mass and receive confirmation in peace, as in not having a baby girl screaming with joy at all the smells, bells, and whistles. She'll get her turn soon enough.

I make this declaration of converted Catholicity knowing right off the bat that it's enough of a revelation

---

THE ACOLYTE

I was concerned
the moment you said
"holy chrism."

---

to arouse suspicion. It would have with me just a year ago, and it may do the same if I hear someone begin a book in this way. A number of assumptions immediately arise in hearing someone make such a declaration, including the potential rigidity of the writer, the amount of identity the writer puts into making sure people know he's Catholic as a convert, and whether or not he's willing to allow dogs to go to heaven. Frankly, you get to ask what this declaration of Catholicity means and intends. That's why you also deserve an explanation, namely, why it's important to how I've written this book, and what you might do with it as you continue reading.

First off, I need to make something clear about myself in relationship to this declaration. I'm really quite grumpy. In fact, I'm downright cantankerous sometimes, and that grouch of a spirit will come out in my writing. I fear that you're likely to associate that surliness with my Catholicity, but please don't. I'm like the third-grumpiest Catholic I know, most of whom I've found to be quite joyful folks. Hollywood may view Catholics as grumpy because Hollywood views *anything* as grumpy that doesn't fit exactly their agenda, but that means nothing about the reality of most Catholics' temperaments. (See! I told you I'm grumpy.) For this reason, I ask a favor: if you read a curmudgeonly statement, don't view it as coming from an old, Catholic man, angry with the world for who knows what—something Catholic, no doubt. View it merely as a nigh middle-aged, confused man, angry with the world for who knows what reason—something food-based, no doubt. I assure you that my anger with the world has nothing to do with my Catholicity and everything to do with my attitude, which is only just learning to be Catholic.

Second, I write this book from a fairly Catholic set of questions, and I fear that you'll think that I've taken up this Catholic method that I do *because* I'm Catholic, say, because I fear excommunication if I don't fall in line. My Catholicity was the endpoint of my journey into the question of God and not a predetermined beginning point. One major reason I converted was because I realized that I was already Catholic in my ways of thinking about God. I became Catholic because I think the tradition gets a lot

---

I'm glad my theology has evolved. I went to an apologetics camp as a teen and we were taught how to witness to Catholics.

THE DEACON

correct intellectually and spiritually. Catholicity was an unexpected destination for me.

This Catholic way of thinking pertains to the way I look at issues surrounding the concept of God. Don't get me wrong; not all the issues that I bring up have anything to do with official Catholic teachings, and much of what I say I've learned from the myriad of other traditions with which I've heartily engaged throughout my life. But the Catholic intellectual tradition generally distinguishes between two ways of talking about God: a way in accordance with *reason* (philosophically) and a way in accordance with *relation* (through faith or theologically). The way of reason brings with it questions about the meaning of the concept of God, why the concept we use is important, and whether that concept has any provable existence beyond, say, my purely wanting it to exist. The way of relation brings with it the question of God's significance for this world and whether God helps out at all, doing something more than merely floating in some eternal ether thinking through just how rad it is to be God.

In general, the distinction I make between a philosopher's God and a God of faith stands at the center of my God-talk, defining the types, manner, and meaning of questions I want to ask. You should simply know this fact as you have other important options for talking about God, even if I believe strongly that they will also have to contend with the one I'm unfolding. Before you render any judgment as to why I present the problems and issues surrounding God in this way, give me a chance to show you why I believe this manner of thinking important.

Rain, Rejection, and Reason

My thoughts on God don't stem from the story of an academic who's been summarily indoctrinated into a certain way of thinking. They stem from my story, and I come to this way of thinking about God conscientiously, seriously, and with a spirit of real inquiry. The reason that the question of God means so much to me stems from the ability of this distinction between the God of faith and reason to bring freedom.

I grew up in Seattle during the grunge era. I still wore sweatpants to school because I was in Middle School, something that I *absolutely* hold against my parents still for letting me do. But I was still in Seattle during the time and definitely old enough to catch the spirit of the age—the *Teen Spirit*, in fact. (Boom!) The demure mood affected everyone who breathed the pot-infused, bleary-eyed, wet, Seattle air.

I don't know a ton about grunge per se, but I remember through songs like Pearl Jam's "Jeremy's Spoken," Nirvana's "Come as You Are," and Soundgarden's "Spoonman" that it always dealt with someone being

---

The title for the Pearl Jam song is "Jeremy." I got the album through the BMG music club and hid it under my bed. P.S. there's an F-bomb in the song.

THE BISHOP

---

socially outcast in a sort of proto-Goth type of way. It
seems to have looked anxiously, defiantly, and with plaid-
covered torsos at the meaninglessness of human life, cri-
tiquing the hordes of obedient persons who bought into
false, hopeful, product-centered beliefs. In other words,
grunge was French existentialism put to music, replacing
cigarettes, coffee, and movies with pot, beer, and dis-
torted guitars.

Seattle was a perfect place for this type of a movement to emerge. It was, after all, a boom-and-bust town
throughout most of its history and started its incline into
a major West Coast population center during the Klon-
dike gold rush. It acted as a shipping and resupply point
on the way to Canada and Alaska for the prospectors
coming from the south and the east. So while its techie-
yuppie feel of today might cover over Seattle's rough,
blue-collar history like bad wallpaper covers over holes
in drywall, Seattle's grounded in the grizzly and god-
less worlds of prospecting, timber-cutting, whoring, and
jet-building (which is *far* more sordid than you think).
Those worlds have stuck with Seattle in the sense that
it's remained one of the most unchurched places in the
country.

I grew up in a place where God was hardly an option
for anyone. My family was semi-religious, but the culture
was not. It was relatively inhospitable to questions of God,
which I don't say to claim that people in Seattle were bad
when I grew up there; not at all! Rather, it's this attitude
that pushed me to search deeply, broadly, and intellectually for any answers in this divine arena. One event in particular eventually forced me into some deep questioning,

which the Seattle-ite in me could not allow to stay at the level of unexamined religious belief.

I introduce this event with a helpful life hint: believing in Jesus doesn't counteract bad health decisions, curing your heart from the effects of a lifetime of smoking and your belly from a lifetime of addiction to pancakes. If it did, the world would convert to the Christian faith by the billions, and we'd all be going to bed with a Slim Jim in one hand, a bag of Cheetos in the other, a Jesus-shaped hole in our hearts sucking all the calories out of these delicious snack-foods like a vacuum picks up loose fur. Nope, belief in Jesus didn't save my father from his bad decisions, and he, me, and my brothers paid the price for his preventable, congestive heart failure.

I lost my father when I was fifteen, just as I stopped wearing sweatpants to school. I needn't get into the difficulty of this loss, especially given my personal closeness to him, but I admit that I still think of him most every day in some manner.

This loss did end up bringing me into the hands of a very loving church family within the Assemblies of God, a charismatic movement that emphasizes the Spirit's call in all things, and a sentiment that I've brought with me wherever I've gone. The church members gave themselves to me as parents, mentors, brothers, sisters, and teachers, withholding from me nothing. I stand forever grateful for their deep charity.

While the love for that community remains, I'm obviously no longer a part of that movement. Part of that stems from the fact that I went to college to become a youth pastor at an Assemblies of God school, which was a saving grace in certain ways and a faith-buster in others. No doubt, very good people worked, taught, and fed me spiritual insight at this school, but I also received a plethora of bad teachings. One of the most prominent of these pertained to a tit-for-tat type of a God, one who would bless you if you first blessed him, which you were usually supposed to do by hearing out and obeying this God's supposedly loving plan for your life. Also, it *felt* like the more people you racked up on the "saved" pile, the more saved you were yourself. This theology produced a crisis for me, which I think is best expressed through *My Name Is Earl*.

Sitcom Truth

I've become a huge fan of this show, and in an especially helpful episode for this particular dilemma, "O Karma, Where Art Thou," Earl runs into a problem. The problem is simple: Earl's conception of Karma isn't working itself out in the way that he thinks it should. Bad things are happening to him, a good person, and good things are happening to his boss, a bad person. I'll back up a bit.

My Name Is Earl is a story of a former petty crook, Earl, and he notices an important pattern in his life: every time something good happens to him, it gets taken away. In the first episode, Earl wins $100,000 from the lotto, immediately gets hit by a car, loses the ticket, and ends up in a hospital where something important happens. He hears Carson Daly—a former MTV VJ for all you young folks—mention something to the effect that good things happen to good people and bad things to bad people, which one of his friends tells him is Karma. He then makes a resolution to right all the wrongs he's done in his

---

How old is too old for Carson Daly? What's a VJ?

THE BISHOP

---

life, which he begins to do by making a list. After getting out of the hospital, Earl finds the lotto ticket again, dedicates the money to righting all his wrongs, and begins to rectify all the bad things he's done, which inevitably produces many hilarious antics.

In the episode in question, Karma isn't doing bad things to the restaurant owner, Mr. Patrick, even though he humiliates his employees, cheats on his wife, and probably kicks dogs. All Earl sees are the wonderful things Mr. Patrick has: a beautiful house, wife, lover, a restaurant of his own, a boat, and some other items that would be uncouth to talk about in a book concerning God. Things shouldn't work this way.

By the end of the episode, Earl socks Mr. Patrick squarely in the face, and we then see Mr. Patrick's body, and then life, go to hell like a row of malcontent dominos. His wife and lover show up at the hospital to check on him at the same time, leading his wife to divorce him and his lover to leave him. He gets booted out of his house, loses his restaurant in the divorce, and even ends up in prison for selling drugs. His life falls apart.

Earl feels bad at first, because rather than fixing something, he destroyed a man's life. Moreover, he believes that he has failed Karma in this situation by not doing something good. He's thrown into an existential crisis. Then Earl's brother, Randy, tells him that maybe Earl acted *for* Karma in this particular instance. Karma used Earl's fist to do its dirty work! Randy's absolutely correct, and the episode ends with a contented Earl drinking beer and knowing things worked out as they should have.

My name is Eric. In college, I found that I had a God-problem. The problem felt a lot like Earl's problem, that the things I had heard about God and the concepts that people have told me about God never added up to how I had experienced God in the real world. After all, in real life things don't work themselves out so cleanly as they do in *My Name Is Earl*, because bad things actually happen to good people and good things actually happen to bad people. Life is arbitrary but God is not, or at least we hope not.

At my college, I was fed the line that God blesses those who bless God. If I was faithful, God would be faithful to me. Of course, bad things had happened to me. I had lost my father, for one thing, and I wondered if it was my fault. After all, God must have preordained it, and most certainly someone was failing in their willingness to bless the good Lord. Perhaps my father died because I hadn't said the magical words "I accept Jesus Christ as my Lord and savior" soon enough. Or perhaps my father secretly cursed the Holy Spirit, putting him in the front line of a divinely inspired death.

A Jewish friend of mine smirkingly claimed on one occasion, "We Jews know there's a God because He does so many evil things to us." Part of his smirk stemmed from the fact that I couldn't tell for sure how serious he was. But the point reminds me of how silly we've gotten with some of our religious ramblings about God, which get so caught up in cultural sentiments, catchphrases, and colloquialisms that the God of relationship can be very difficult to take seriously.

Catchphrase theology is the leading cause of eye rolls in the church.

THE ELDER

That's where the God of reason became freeing for me, and that's why I took up a search for it fulltime. The cynical, grunge-driven Seattle-ite in me needed better answers, and I couldn't just buy into the common culture of disbelieving in God without becoming like those who I viewed with some contempt at the time: weak-willed people who weren't willing to search for answers to difficult questions. I was driven beyond the religious and secular cultures to which I had become accustomed, and I rejected their dismissal of the application of reason to God, taking up the question of God as an intellectual pursuit. The God of reason became for me a flashlight in a dark room where I could earlier *smell* that someone was hiding a dead, rotting fish—maybe even several—but couldn't yet find it. No, without the light of the philosopher's God, I'd have no hope of ferreting out these smelly mackerels of falsehood, and I had zero chance of ever finding anything like truth about God. Luckily, I found myself a flashlight in philosophy.

A Catholic Method, but an Open Conversation

Like I said, I talk about God in a very Catholic way in this book, and I take this Catholic embrace of God, which ascribes deep importance to the God of reason, to be anything but dogmatic: it's totally and completely freeing and has liberated my thoughts from the culture Christianity that holds sway in almost all arenas. To seek out and embrace the God of reason has been nothing but a boon for my spiritual life and how I think theologically.

Still, I don't write or think about this God of reason as an endpoint, the consummation of all proper God ideas. It presents a beginning point, and the polarizing-for-many-but-very-important Pope Benedict has something important to say in this regard:

> This God of the philosophers, whose pure eternity and unchangeability had excluded any relation with the changeable and transitory, now appeared to the eye of faith as the God of men, who is not only the thought of all thoughts, the eternal mathematics of the universe, but also *agape*, the power of creative love.[1]

The God of reason cannot be the end of our thoughts about God from a Christian standpoint, and I am very much Christian. The God of reason eventually has to be reconceived *relationally*. While the God of reason must help us to sift through the wheat and the chaff of our theological lives, we must also recognize that without the beautiful relationship we call faith, God simply doesn't matter except in the most intellectually abstract ways. Intellectual abstraction is important, but not enough.

In this regard, I'm writing this book to a twenty-year-old me. I want him to know some stuff that $30K in student loans, poor life-decisions, marrying an awesome woman, reading lots of dead people, holding my first baby, and becoming aware of my impending death taught me about God and my issues with the concept, only I want my twenty-year-old self to have this wisdom without all the trouble. I want to show him a different path into the beauty of reflecting reasonably on God that he didn't know was available at the time, and I want show him the dignity of the limitations that our thoughts on God eventually succumb to in relation. I want my twenty-year-old self to know God philosophically and theologically, conceptually and spiritually, even if I only concentrate on the philosophical and conceptual for the most part. Alas, I doubt I'll listen.

To this end, I owe an answer to the question of why my Catholicity shouldn't be off-putting for the suspicious, and the answer's simple. For one, we all speak from where we are, and I'm no different. I speak from the standpoint of the tradition that I had embraced intellectually far

---

As long as where you are doesn't dismiss where I am, I am down to listen.

THE ACOLYTE

---

before I embraced it spiritually. Second, the fact of my standpoint doesn't mean that the book's catholicity makes it exclusively for Catholics. Rather, I think the Catholic method used to talk about God in this book can be entered into a broader conversation, helping anyone who's interested in gaining freedom from their theological baggage, even if only by showing these persons how much they disagree with me! I'm good with that.

God Is Not a Cosmic Vending Machine

We all know that God looks like a shredded Old-Man River. We've seen this image a thousand times. Michelangelo gave it to us in the Vatican fresco, showing God stretching himself out to touch (or maybe pull) Adam's finger. Bearded, gray-haired, male, eighty-six years old, and usually just a little bit pissed off at you: those seem to be the main characteristics of God.

The image is not alone; they never are alone in our thinking. We also pair this image with a definition of God: a cosmic vending machine. Into this vending machine, you have to put the right change to get the goods of your heart's desire: recite magical incantations using the right prayers, be sorry enough for leering too long at your neighbor's new MacBook, or do magical, God-pleasing deeds, and you'll get something in return. Shredded

Old-Man River will look down on you with a sense of calculated favor, giving you your heart's desire: marriage, a new car, or even that massage you want so badly from a David Hasselhoff lookalike.

THE DEACON

I just YouTubed Hasselhoff and lost two hours of my life.

Images and definitions tend to develop in light of each other, which is what we see in this portrayal of God. Images yield for us certain definitions because they focus our attention on certain features of the object we want to understand. In the above case, it's God's seeming volatile demeanor and cheap ability to buy off. Definitions, in turn, draw from the reality of these images, tease out the reality of the image, and then cement how we come to interpret these images, which is why we attempt to please and even manipulate this volatility with magical incantations and cosmic coins. This play between concept and image can set us on a virtuous path, a path that opens us up further to the reality of what we're trying to talk about, or it can set us on a vicious path, enclosing us within our images and their associated definitions and preventing us from possibly thinking anything more beneficial, real, or true. So it is with our usual understanding of God, which has become stifling. We need to free up the idea of God by addressing the mess of images and concepts that we've come to associate with it. We need to get out from underneath Old

---

If fear or greed isn't the
motivation, I wonder
how many people would
really care about God?

THE ELDER

Man River's storm cloud and stop putting change into the
cosmic vending machine. To do so, we'll need some new
images and concepts.

I present to you the new pantheon.

Mr. Miyagi, the God of Classical Theism

We don't generally run into randomly burning bushes on
our hikes. If we do, our first call is to the National Forest
Service, who can summon a helicopter to drop a massive,
airborne bucket of water on the bush. Moses didn't have
this option, so when he ran into a burning bush in the
Sinai desert, he investigated, and it turns out that the bush
started talking to him. It was God.

At the time, Moses had essentially been running
from the Egyptians after killing an Egyptian taskmas-
ter. He found a wife and father-in-law in the desert, and
was merrily living out his days as a shepherd, singing to
sheep and tickling goats. He was happy, that is, until the
Almighty caught up with him in the form of a burning
bush. Through the bush, God commands Moses to go and
lead the Israelites out of Egypt, and Moses asks on what
authority he will do such a thing. The Lord responds,

"If I come to the Israelites and say to them, 'The God of your ancestors has sent me to you,' and they ask me, 'What is his name?' what shall I say to them?" God said to Moses, "I am who I am." He said further, "Thus you shall say to the Israelites, 'I am has sent me to you.'" God also said to Moses, "Thus you shall say to the Israelites, 'The LORD, the God of your ancestors, the God of Abraham, the God of Isaac, and the God of Jacob, has sent me to you':

"This is my name forever,
     and this my title for all generations."[1]

The divine name of the Lord, "I am," is revealed, and on the grounds of the power of this name, Moses is to lead the Israelites.

In terms of a definition of God, classical theists have used this passage as a way of biblically depicting the concept of God that they describe. *God is.* God is, in fact, identical with this *is*, and we need to learn what that means. For that task, we turn to Mr. Miyagi.

I first saw *The Karate Kid* some years after it came out, when I was around eight years old. I *loved* that movie. The idea that you could take on a group of powerful bullies provoked the same awe in me then that I now have toward Captain America. Surprisingly, I actually didn't give a crap about Daniel-san. He was necessary for the plotline, but even as a grade-schooler I thought him a bit over-the-top. Instead, I bowed before the altar of Mr. Miyagi. Little did I know that in *The Karate Kid*, I was learning theology, for Miyagi represents the classical concept of God, defined by equanimity, patience, and thoughtfulness. Even though all the new, sexy, show-off concepts pick on this concept given Miyagi's seeming unathletic, older, and shorter demeanor, Miyagi isn't easily angered, moved, or provoked. But mess with him too much, and Miyagi will reverse the crap out of your punches and kick you in the face.

Although it's not in the movie, I like to imagine that Mr. Miyagi worked for the Department of Transportation at some point. It fits given his penchant for old cars. In my mind's eye, he was a topographical surveyor, and he surely had to earn the respect of his semi-racist, macho crew of

---

Mr. Miyagi running the DMV might be the best idea yet.

THE DEACON

---

co-workers who called themselves Highway-Ki. He did this in a one-on-seven group fight, which ended with Miyagi spin-kicking the crew-leader in the ribs, then helping him up. These details aside, we can learn a lot about Miyagi as a concept of God from Mr. Miyagi's (hypothetical) days of surveying.

When surveying topographically, you need a stable point from which to take all measurements, since you're trying to create a map that will define the low points and high points in your allotted territory. If you measure the height of a bump from one spot and the depth of a dip from another, you need to know the difference between the first point of measurement and the second in order to gain an accurate measurement of the bump and dip. The Miyagi-God is this stable point of measurement.

Miyagi-God intertwines heavily with our views of knowledge and reality. Ancient philosophers rightly thought that in order to know anything, you need to find a stable point of reference from which to measure all things. If you want to find out whether a wall is plumb, you use a plumbline, which uses the stability of gravity to measure the crookedness of the wall. Similarly, if you want to know what a dog is, what a table is, or what a word is, then you need one concept undergirding all others and offering them the means by which to exist as their particular identity. No stability, no identity. Miyagi-God is that stability point, an absolute identity undergirding all things in the world. Because of this stability point, you can make a topographical map of the world in which you live. You can measure the difference between the hills and valleys of our worlds and know that those measurements are correct.

Through Miyagi-God, we come to measure nature and how things in this world function, which we can do because this world is encoded with the very essence of Miyagi-God's intellect. In a well-known scene that made us all want to help our parents wash their cars, Mr. Miyagi teaches Daniel-san karate by way of car waxing. "Wax on; wax off," Miyagi says. After weeks of Daniel-san waxing Miyagi's sweet set of classical cars, the boy gets mad. He accuses Mr. Miyagi of taking advantage of him and asking when he's going to teach him karate. Miyagi responds by throwing a couple of punches at Daniel-san, and Daniel blocks the punches using the "wax on; wax off" technique. Mr. Miyagi built into Daniel-san the proper habits of karate-based blocking through car waxing!

I tried to appropriate this pedagogical technique to no avail. My kids told me they were pacifists and weren't comfortable training to fight.

THE ELDER

Miyagi-God pulls a similar move with this world by building into each creature a set of rational habits that's shared with all similar creatures—without these creatures even having to touch Carnuba! These habits give each creature a set of divinely inspired natural directives— a "nature"—that allow the creature to live and thrive within the world. So, cows have a cow nature and moo because of it (moo on, moo off); humans have a human nature and think because of it; and we can only think through each of these natures truthfully because Miyagi acts as the standard and measure through which we see and think. Nature, which is the comprehensive relationship of all particular natures to one another, is Miyagi-God's divine blueprint for the world and a reflection of the divine intellect.

Importantly, Miyagi-God affirms this natural order of things and never oversteps his natural, intellectual bounds with it. Even more so, Miyagi *can't* overstep these bounds because, strangely, Miyagi-God's essence as absolute identity puts limits on him. For instance, some God-concepts envision God as being able to make 2 and 2 equal

5, but that's only with versions of God where the answer to 2 and 2 is decided on by an ultimate being. From the standpoint of Miyagi-God, this equation isn't decided upon—it merely represents and flows from Miyagi's divinely reasonable being in the same way that a stream flows from a glacier.

THE ACOLYTE

So I am guessing I shouldn't ask about God making a car so big you can't wax all of it?

This idea obviously rejects what we often call "omnipotence," at least in the sense of God being able to do whatever God wants. Miyagi-God can only do what is consistent with God's constant and perfect identity, which can seem a bit confusing. Miyagi-omnipotence comes to mean that God always acts in the highest, most noble, and beautiful ways possible, which is consistent with God's nature as the highest reality. So, Miyagi-God can't interact with creation whimsically, changing the rules of the

---

THE DEACON

Why should God's power be limited by God's character? Shouldn't it be directed by God's character?

---

universe out of his grumpiness because of some cheap, take-out-inspired, divine indigestion. He can't act in contradiction to the reason that flows from him, of which the world is a direct and created reflection.

I have so many conversations in which people think God CAN BE and IS against them.  **THE BISHOP** For God to have a consistently loving character, we have to reread quite a few Bible passages.

This way of thinking about God is very distinct from the God we think we've come to know, and Miyagi-God yet has one final surprise up his sleeve. Miyagi, while in certain ways totally and completely distinct from you, is also the very energy in which you and all other things exist. Spoiler alert for an '80s movie: Mr. Miyagi heals Daniel-san toward the end of the movie, giving Daniel-san the power to go on and win the local karate tournament. He heals him by way of some sort of Eastern magic, the movie semi-racistly implies, and we all bought it because, frankly, we were semi-racists in the '80s. Anyway, Mr. Miyagi is able somehow to tie himself into the energy animating this world, using it to heal Daniel-san for this local sporting event. If I'm to analyze this scene now, I must believe that he's tying himself into his namesake's God, who is the very life-giving energy of this world, the Being who brings a pulse to the lifeblood of the cosmos. After all, Miyagi-God isn't merely some distant and untouched reality; Miyagi-God is the one in whom we exist, move, and have our being.[2] Miyagi-God undergirds our every act as the force that sustains our existence.

I think that's exactly what the movie's creators had in mind.

Trying to get our minds around Miyagi-God can be frustrating. An image beyond *The Karate Kid* helps. I have on my wall a painting by the famous (at least by Montana standards) Charlie Russell, a cowpoke, artist, and story-teller who drew his experiences in the Montana west. The image is of three members of the Blackfeet tribe, long before their capture and internment on a reservation. One man, his eyes closed and face tilted upward, sits on his horse, his hands raised toward the morning sun. The others sit around him in solemn and respectful silence. The painting is called *Sun Worshippers*.

The sun forms a helpful traditional experience—one that we can directly access in our everyday life—used to help experience Miyagi-God more directly. Many beyond the Blackfeet have used it, and the reason for the use of this image is simple: the sun forms the source of the world's life. It lends to the world the light, heat, and sus-tenance necessary for the world to work. It allows all the plants of the earth to grow, heats the skin of the animals that need these plants to survive, and shines light on the prey that the predator will not otherwise see. Miyagi-God acts as the light-giving sun of our mind's eye; he is the substance or quality that allows us to grasp all truth and meaning. Even more so, just as the sun creates life, gives life, sustains life, Miyagi-God is the ether of our existence, the medium through whom we exist.

Almost any philosophical theologian prior to 1300 CE will buy into some basic notion of God as Miyagi, including pagans (Plato and Plotinus), Christians (Augustine, Gregory of Nyssa, and Thomas Aquinas), Jews (Maimonides), and Muslims (Avicenna and Averroes). Any which way these thinkers develop the particulars, "God" stands for the highest, animating concept that imbues the world with meaning, identity, and life. All things come to exist through Miyagi-God, depending on him for their continued existence.

In sum, Miyagi is the source and end of all things, the most potent act of being, and the geometry of the universe. He is the absolute intellect that forms all things and sets forth a reasonable order, allowing his creatures to function with their built-in GPS systems. As such, Miyagi-God is like a father—or a martial arts instructor—who gives his child (creation) the car and money to go on a date without following the child throughout the date. He's also awesome in that he'll be waiting to drive off any motorcycle-riding gangs of bullies who come to ruin your good time.

Jersey Shore, the God of Voluntarism

In the horrific biblical book called Judges, filled as it is with rape, dismemberment, and destruction, one story in particular stands out to me: that of Jephthah. You see, Jephthah was a mighty warrior whom the Israelites turned to in a time of need to deliver them by war from their enemies, the Ammonites. He made a promise to God that, should God give him the Ammonites, he'd sacrifice the first thing that came out to greet him on his return home.

THE BISHOP

Why should any story start this way!?!

> Then Jephthah came to his home at Mizpah; and there was his daughter coming out to meet him with timbrels and with dancing. She was his only child; he had no son or daughter except her. When he saw her, he tore his clothes, and said, "Alas, my daughter! You have brought me very low; you have become the cause of great trouble to me. For I have opened my mouth to the Lord, and I cannot take back my vow."[3]

And Jephthah didn't take back his vow. And God seemed to have accepted his bounty. And this is problematic! Welcome to the Jersey Shore of god-concepts, who is just as problematic and the likely source of our understanding of God as Old-Man Vending Machine.

I have a confession to make. I'm not proud of it, but my wife and I watched a full season of *Jersey Shore* when it first came out. It's almost as addictive as cheese steaks. It was a strange experience because we didn't actually like the show; we simply got sucked into the strange world of orange skin, partying, and hair spray. Frankly, I think the show made us feel better about ourselves because we could look at this morally calloused group of individuals

If you were younger
you would know the
entire reality show
can be the antagonist
for the engaged viewer in community.
#ITweetThroughTheBachelor

THE ACOLYTE

and know that, heck, at least we were better than a few
people out there in the world!

The show's characters were consumed by their immediate and animal desires. It seemed as though no frontal lobe of the brain had developed in any of them—you know, the part of the brain that actually makes us human. So it is with the Jersey-Shore-God, a smack-talking, desire-driven, and completely unpredictable God who most certainly has orange skin, a bad drinking habit, and no control over his temper. He probably also smells like stale cigarettes. This Jersey Shore-God has zero impulse control and a rationality at the service of desire, and he most definitely regularly gets into fights over "whose beer that is."

The problem they had
with beer was not *whose*,
but the tasteless *what*
they put in their mouth.
#PBRistheBEERcalvin

THE DEACON

What I'm asking is that you please just stay out of Jersey Shore-God's hot tub.

There's really only one scene from the whole of *Jersey Shore* that I remember with any sort of clarity, the rest falling into a beer-induced haze. Ronnie, who was always either elbow deep into a pull-up or in an argument with his girlfriend, was wandering the boardwalk with his debate-partner, Sammy Sweetheart. Some other equally well-adjusted gentleman began to pick a fight with him. The machismo leading up to the fight was one of the funniest things I've seen. Two drunken sailors began sizing each other up with Ronnie yelling: "Come at me, bro! Come at me!" A brief, nonlethal, and even nonpainful-looking fight took place, after which we see Ronnie running down the street away from the scuffle back to his home, like a massive, inebriated toddler.

Whereas Mr. Miyagi lives a thoughtful life—he is intentional, putting his desires to the test of reason before acting on those desires—the Jersey Shore folks live in a different situation. (Wink.) That's why Miyagi kicks so

---

5 points! #TheSituation

THE ACOLYTE

---

much butt without ever hurting anyone too badly! While he might desire to hurt someone, he doesn't think it's right. Desire is always a function of intellect for Miyagi, which isn't the case for Jersey Shore-God.

For the crew on *Jersey Shore*, intellect functions solely at the discretion of any desires they may have. When hungry, they will use their intellects as a tool to find a way to get food; when thirsty, they will do the same to get beer; when randy, well, do the math. Like Ronnie on the boardwalk, the whole of the *Jersey Shore* cast seems merely to meander their way through life, searching drunkenly for more burritos and Miller. I'm not saying that they don't have intellects, but I am saying that their intellects only serve their wills.

With the Jersey-Shore-God, much the same takes place. Intellect takes the backburner. Intellect solely serves the will, which really comes to be the primary characteristic of the Jersey Shore-God. He doesn't govern through a natural blueprint. No shared natures among creatures exist in Jersey Shore-God's world. The Jersey Shore-God governs the world directly, taking a very hands-on approach to each and every individual thing. Rather than giving creatures the freedom to enact their natures as they see fit, Jersey Shore-God gets directly into everyone's business.

I'm saying that Jersey Shore-God is a close-talker and will definitely fight you if you don't do what his alcohol-laden breath has to say.

I imagine that if you're unfortunate enough to gain an invite to the *Jersey Shore* home, these are the first words you'll hear: "My house—my rules." The old saying actually has a benign, live-and-let-live connotation, but in the mouths of the *Jersey Shore* cast, it's an excuse for them to do whatever sordid things they want to do. It's also the basic meaning of the philosophical term *voluntarism*, which means that you can do what you want. In the context of Jersey Shore-God, it refers to omnipotence. Jersey Shore-God's house—which is all of creation—Jersey Shore-God's rules.

Because Jersey Shore-God is a will who creates each thing individually and without a nature, he has no blueprint to keep it in check. Only from Jersey Shore God-concept do we get ideas like that of God making 2 and 2 equal 5, or a God creating square circles. Similarly, only from the standpoint of *Jersey Shore* do we get skeptical questions as to whether God can create a rock so big that God cannot lift it. All these ideas and questions tend to make sense within Jersey Shore because, in this God, there exists no intellectual nature or divine blueprint for the world; there exists only Jersey Shore's will, which is absolutely oriented toward beer and tacos.

THE ACOLYTE

You have failed to answer the real question: how many trips to the tanning bed does it take to get the perfect *The Jersey Shore* bronze? #WeMayNeverKnow

---

And don't tell me that this isn't the case given some of the crazy sacrifices an obviously hungry god demands of his people such as fatted calves and goats. He may as well have added that the Israelites give him a tortilla, too! Darker yet is the possibility that there lies no other way to justify the many horrific genocides, cleansings, and otherwise atrocious acts we find God commanding biblically than by saying that Jersey Shore creates the standards of morality not based on his ever-steady being but his whims.

Late medieval Catholic philosophical theologians such as Duns Scotus and William of Ockham developed this conception of God because of the stifling forms of scholasticism that had emerged at the time, and it became the popular conception with many of the Reformers. For Martin Luther, John Calvin, and Huldrych Zwingli, God was an absolute, unpredictable, and all-powerful will. They were terrified of this God apart from the revelation on the cross, which was the only reason they thought that God could be trusted.

In fact, Luther, a theologian whom I very much adore, has a real problem because he insisted that God is both revealed and hidden. He's revealed on the cross, which Luther claims depicts the love that God has for us, but God's hiddenness remains, and it remains a very big conundrum. Of course, any decent god-concept will contain divine mystery, but mystery for Luther is scarier than most. He asks whether mystery is something you can trust, like Daniel-san could trust the mysterious ways of Miyagi's training style, or whether something scary and wrathful underlies this mystery, giving God a split personality whose darkness comes out drunk, pissed, and swinging. For all the emphasis on grace in Luther, he couldn't shake the idea that God might just kick back a few too many and bring with him a belligerent imitation of justice whose only rationale can be seen from a God surfing atop a speeding Camaro and yelling, "I can do it cause I'm God, baby! Wooooooo!"

More importantly, for those of us who live in the twenty-first-century United States, there's a good chance that Jersey Shore is part of our assumed God-repertoire, coming to us by way of extreme Calvinism. We know this God whenever something bad happens to us, and we immediately ask ourselves whether God's punishing us for something. We also know it whenever something good happens to us, and we lead ourselves to believe that, for no reason other than grace, God has blessed us—although we suspect that God will want something from us soon. For this reason, we need to think through and understand exactly what makes up this God, as it has characteristics that we today take as rote fact but from which we need to free ourselves. This God, after all, isn't much different than pure chance.

Retired Oprah, the God of Deism

We get so mixed up in creationism ideologies these days that a lot of folks don't realize that Genesis has two, very different creation accounts. The first account concludes with the following statement:

> Thus the heavens and the earth were finished, and all their multitude. And on the seventh day God finished the work that he had done, and he rested on the seventh day from all the work that he had done. So God blessed the seventh day and hallowed it, because on it God rested from all the work that he had done in creation.[4]

From what I know of an absolutely insane field of study in biblical studies called source criticism, the first creation account is written by a Priestly community during the Southern Kingdom's captivity in Babylon. It not only counters and corrects some of the images of the Babylonian creation account in the *Enuma Elish*, which prioritizes violence over peace, but it claims that the God of Israel has Lordship over all other gods and the whole of creation. God is sovereign over Babylonian gods and, thus, the God of Israel, Lord on high, caused Israel's capture, not Babylon.

These initial accounts in Genesis emphasize a particular distance of God from creation, which is the closest we get in biblical texts to a god-concept called deism. And the God of Deism is Oprah, but retired. The only problem with this metaphor is that deism's followers worship their God far less than Oprah's followers worship her. At any rate, Oprah built for herself a massive business and media empire piece by piece, amassing a fortune along the way. She battled through what was likely a racist and sexist industry only to emerge pretty much on the top of the thing, Mario-stomping the adversity that sought to prevent her success along the way. Upon this empire, Oprah seems to have retired and set up a bunch of charitable businesses, hiring managers to run both those and her empire. Oprah herself no doubt opts for drinking mimosas on her Caribbean estate while Steadman gives her foot massages.

Spoiler Alert! Oprah is not divine. She's the charismatic leader of a massive corporation. Although Oprah's corporation doesn't structurally depend on her for its continued functioning, she acts as a necessary component within it, making important decisions, enacting company rules, and simply being who she is: its Pontiac-giving, show-hosting boss.

Miyagi-God is a life-giving act of identity. Jersey Shore-God potentially functions as Miyagi does, but acts as an unchecked will in the process. Oprah-God merely represents one person in a vast and complicated conglomerate. She is a person among other persons, even if she's the most important, meaning she stands on a continuum with all other beings in creation. If the zebra sits below the human being on this continuum of worldly existence, Oprah sits at the top, sort of like a super-being.

THE DEACON

Growing up, my minister said Oprah's book club was cult propagating a false gospel with a smile.

Miyagi and Jersey Shore are what we'd call "omnipresent." Because they are *in* all things, they are present to all things everywhere. Oprah-God is not. She doesn't necessarily exist in space and time, but she does exist as a being among fellow beings, the head honcho among lower, less powerful personnel.

I'm no business guru, but I've heard one thing about creating a business that I'll happily relay to you: one of the most important parts of running a successful business is found in its procedures. They allow you to have persons of all kinds of intellectual capacity, from smart to stupid, who know and have a manner of dealing with any situation as it arises to the benefit of the company. My guess is that Oprah's multinational holds to this rule at a far more complex level.

So does the Oprah-God's creation hold to the same rule. The world follows and abides by a strict set of procedures, which are absolutely rational, and you can know them only by way of the intellect, especially as found in the empirical sciences. No one can break these rules, not even Oprah-God herself. Once set up, these rules abide and run themselves without any divine interference. In this way, Oprah can hire just about any bonehead, and this employee cannot screw up the company.

From the perspective of the Oprah-God, these laws represent the laws of nature. Nature is absolute from this perspective, and its rules, regulations, and patterns show no signs of being broken in her worldly corporation. Neither, however, are these rules analogous to how we might think of them with Miyagi-God—as in him and sustained by him. They are simply the corporate structure, and they stand absolutely separate from Oprah except as the rules of the world. She stands outside of them as their creator, able to retire to Tahiti while reaping their benefits.

We can find this Oprah-God difficult to associate with any experience given the distance between her and us, but I think you'll find something of this God all over the place in the U.S.: "In God We Trust" is on our currency, and "under God" is in the Pledge of Allegiance. I have no qualms with either because I don't care enough to take an interest. But then Jeb Bush, in the run-up to the 2016 election, said, "I think religion ought to be about making us better as people, less about things [that] end up getting into the political realm."[5] This sentiment we'll no doubt find on both sides of the political aisle in the U.S., and it represents the Retired Oprah-God position really well: keep God out of politics, which can now operate by way of the sciences of economics and political analysis, but acknowledge the God who sets the objects of these sciences up and implements their order in the world. God's there somewhere, but you certainly don't need to disturb her martini-filled rest on this seventh day.

That we find Oprah-God in the U.S. political system makes a lot of sense. Some of the most famous deists come from Britain, the U.S., and France. They include John Locke, Thomas Jefferson, Benjamin Franklin, and Jean-Jacques Rousseau. Arguably, German thinkers such as Immanuel Kant also bought into this Oprah-God concept. These thinkers, all of whom sought reprieve from what they considered the machinations of the church and organized religion as a whole, found this view of God freeing. After all, the most famous image of a deistic God comes from the idea of a clockmaker: she creates the clock, including all the mechanisms that allow it to function and continue keeping time; she then winds the clock, lets it go, and moves on to some drinks by her lonesome. The Oprah-God simply leaves the world alone, providing a buffer between those who want to enact a functioning society by way of the newly emergent social sciences, and those who dogmatically claim to know God's revelatory will.

Your Grandparents' Pantheon

We now have your grandparents' pantheon set up. I say your grandparents' pantheon because Oprah forms the newest of these ideas, and she historically pops up as a popular God-idea within the seventeenth century. This time is otherwise known as way before you were born, as the time, in fact, that the U.S. and modern France were emerging. In these concepts, we have a God who's seen as absolute intellect (Miyagi), one who's seen as absolute will (Jersey Shore), and a final one who's seen as literally out of this world (Oprah). To no small degree, parts and aspects of these visions of God remain with us today. Still, out of fairness, we need to lower the average age of our pantheon and begin searching for a couple of God-concepts with fewer mothballs in their coat pockets.

Not Your Grandparents' Pantheon

My wife and I went to visit one of our grandparents a little after getting married. (For confidentiality and out of sincere love, I will not say whom.) We had a great conversation about everything from the right proportion of mayo/tuna in a tuna sandwich (a *lot* of mayo, according to Gramma, and I totally agree) to cleaning gutters safely. Then Gramma, a good and beautiful woman, began talking about her hair salon, how long she'd gone there, and what the "illegals" are doing to their town according to the folks at the salon. My wife sat straight up, cringed, and tried to redirect the conversation back to family and old memories. We succeeded, dropping politics to look at old photo albums where we got back the Gramma we love.

The comedian Bill Burr has a hilarious bit about these moments and our reactions to them, which he brought up after the *Duck Dynasty* guy, Phil Robertson, and the Clippers' owner, Donald Sterling, got into trouble with the media over some bigotry:

> And I'm not saying what these people did wasn't offensive. . . . What pissed me off was at no point during all of these stories did anyone address their age. They're old! What did you *think* they thought? You've never talked to a grandparent and asked the wrong question and all of the sudden you went down this crazy road? I'm gonna be honest with you, too: people were too hard on that Clippers' guy, man. . . . For an 80-year-old white guy, that wasn't that bad. He didn't drop the N-word *once*, and that's unbelievable for an 80-year-old white guy![1]

If strong language, a complete lack of a PC filter, and utter hilariousness don't bother you, go watch the rest for yourself.

If we're serious about our religious life, we need to know the pantheon we've discussed so far. Just as we wouldn't get through an old photo album without our grandparents' stories, we won't be able to get very far in the further study of god without it. But the mildly racist comments can get a little old at times, so we may also need to find some gods our own age, some gods who drink PBR tall boys and call pizza "flat bread"; some gods who, whatever else they think about immigration, don't sum the life of the person up as an "illegal."

Two gods fit this bill, and they've really found their footing in the nineteenth and twentieth centuries; they'll have illustrious careers. Both gods, moreover, will actively depend on the assumptions associated with the more classical concepts of God while calling them into question. By assumptions, I mean ideas like our grandparents' views about computers. These gods are, of course, your Hippie Aunt and Joan of Arc.

Your Hippie Aunt, the God of Process Theology

According to the Gospel of John, "The Word became flesh and lived among us, and we have seen his glory, the glory as of a father's only son, full of grace and truth."[2] The Word—the second person of the Trinity and the one whom the ancients proclaim as one being with the father—*became* flesh. If we take this word "became" seriously, then it seems that God changes, becomes something other than what God already was. In this case, God takes on human form. This idea is in diametric opposition to our previous concepts of God, in which God doesn't *become* but simply *is*—gods who don't change but simply remain the same—and it's this notion of God amidst change that we need to take up.

Your hippie aunt, who very recently entered the online dating world, loves farmers' markets, patchouli oil, and kale. She definitely went to UC-Berkeley in the '60s and earned a journalism degree, sitting in on any number of the raucous protests during the time. She also loved the original idea of Burning Man festival, but looks down on it now that it's been taken over by yuppie-techie types. She's somehow worked as a freelance poet since college and has absolutely no trust in conventional ideas of marriage. She hates both Bushes (41 and 43), and she regularly engages in drum circles on the street corner protesting various causes. She's your quirky but kind, free-loving but intelligent, hippie aunt.

THE DEACON

My aunt was not a hippie. She's head of the Women's Missionary Union and local NRA chapter.

Your aunt discovered Tai Chi in the '80s while everyone else focused on gyms. Instead of bulky muscles, she was interested in her body having the right energy and flow, becoming a part of the world around her, and maintaining its plasticity even while aging. When she heard about this Eastern practice, she took it up immediately. You'll now see her in the park every morning in a red sweatsuit with a rainbow bandana, fluidly performing her katas and making herself at one with the rising sun.

The Hippie Aunt-God also exists in a perpetual state of Tai Chi-ing. She moves in a constant state of mutually conditioning flow with the world. She has no stagnancy to her, and no absolute or static identity. Like the retired Oprah-God, she is the greatest being in the cosmos. Unlike Oprah, she hasn't retired to a distant island to allow the world to work its own problems out. No, Hippie Aunt-God relates to the world just as your hippie aunt sits in a nonchlorinated hot spring: immersed in and flowing with, but still separable from that hot spring; she's at one with the hot spring and relationally defined by it but not simply identical to the water within in it.

I am feeling awkwardly
comfortable with her.

THE BISHOP

Your hippie aunt had a child in 1975 with her life-partner, Joel. Having raised a child mostly by herself, she'll tell you all day long that rules and structure can really stifle a child's freedom and creativity, which is why she always let Moonstar, your cousin, explore herself and the world as she saw fit. Sometimes this parenting technique led to some eye-rollingly awful scenarios, like when Moonstar joined an interpretive dance troupe. Other times it led to some unexpectedly cool results, like when Moonstar mastered the sitar.

Hippie Aunt-God also refuses to put too much structure into the world—she considers Miyagi-God a domineering dictator. Nor does she plan each second of the world's life as does Jersey Shore-God, getting in the world's face and picking a fight. For Hippie Aunt-God, the world is free to become whatever it wants and to evolve as it sees fit. In fact, Hippie Aunt-God will evolve her parenting style right alongside the world's choices. Maybe unlike your human hippie aunt, though, Hippie Aunt-God will not merely let her children run amok with no structures whatsoever; she will try to call the world to its best possibilities, which are generally defined by peace, love, and the spontaneous relationships that emerge from these qualities.

Your human hippie aunt likes few activities better than a good drum circle. If it takes place as a protest, even better! As she says, "You get so many different people with so many different stories and so many different drums playing together in one, beautiful, and spontaneous rhythm." There emerges a unity within the diversity of people involved, and that whole rhythm constantly evolves through each person's individual evolutions. For Hippie Aunt-God, this truth develops on any number of cosmic levels. For one, all the beings—their lives and natural movements—in the world form the members of a drum circle. The rhythm itself *is* the world, which emerges from all the relationships of the beings keeping the beat.

THE ELDER

The idea of a churchwide cosmic drum circle and yoga session is not cool. We should stick with robes and skip the stretch pants.

As with the beings of the world, so too with the religions of the world. For Hippie Aunt-God, religion itself is one giant, cosmic drum circle. She takes the lead drum, of course, but Jesus, the Buddha, Mohammed, and Krishna all join in, trying to get all the other beings in the world into the benign cosmic rhythm that she is leading. When all religions drum together, weaving their rhythms in and out of one another, all beings in the world follow in her flow.

Coca Cola tried to leverage this idea in its 1970s commercial, where the world unites around drinking carbonated, high-fructose corn syrup. The concept comes to light in reality in devastating moments like 9/11 or the recent Paris terrorist attacks. In the midst of utter chaos and at a time when the rest of the world says we should all be turning against each other and fighting for our own individual survival, the world coalesces into an unexpected unity instead. The very world that should be thrown into disarray finds its better possibility, coming to enact the world as it should have always been to begin with: in loving relationship. Even if this coalescence (concrescence, in process terms) is momentary, it attests to the real possibility of this God and her importance.

Philosophers such as Alfred Whitehead and Charles Hartshorne made this concept of God famous throughout the late nineteenth, twentieth, and into the 21st centuries, and more recently, theologians such as John Cobb, Marjorie Suchocki, and David Ray Griffin baptized this god into Christian and Truther circles. Her followers today are interested in ecological, economic, social-justice, and 9/11 issues, and the ways that our relationships with our world and each other can cause good, harm, or government conspiracies. For all of these theologians, Hippie Aunt-God stands for a relational god-concept, inherently critical of the isolated and so-called nonrelational god-concepts that came before her.

What needs to be taken from this idea is that Hippie Aunt-God's identity is not merely her own, but she shares herself and her patchouli with the world. She allows this world to remain free while calling it always to its best possibilities. For Hippie Aunt-God, the drum circle definitely forms the world's best possibilities. In that drum circle, all the world, including God, can enter into a beautiful unity that respects diversity.

Joan of Arc and the God of Hermeneutics

In 1 Corinthians, St. Paul makes a famous statement:

> For the message about the cross is foolishness to
> those who are perishing, but to us who are being
> saved it is the power of God. For it is written,
>
> > I will destroy the wisdom of the wise,
> > > and the discernment of the discerning I
> > > will thwart . . .
>
> For God's foolishness is wiser than human
> wisdom, and God's weakness is stronger than
> human strength.[3]

God, according to Paul, is really into breaking our expectations, be it the expectations of his fellow Jews' demands
for signs, such as Thomas's demand to see Christ's
wounds, or the Gentiles' demands for Greek wisdom:
that God exists very distantly from us, unconcerned
with the smallness of our world. God, says Paul, is in
the business of defying our demands and upsetting our
expectations, and it's precisely here that we find the final
god-concept: that of the hermeneutic God. (FYI, *hermeneutics* is simply a fancy word for interpretation.) AKA,
Joan of Arc-God.

The world of military power and strategy hasn't historically lent itself to equal opportunity values, but we can
find a number of exceptions to this, and the most famous
is Joan of Arc. Born to a peasant family, she received religious visions that set her on a path to help the French
military win back its land and crown from the English.
Normalcy did not define this path for Joan. For instance,

we can imagine the shock for the mayor of the city of Auxerre who, after he parlayed his capitulation to French rule,
realized that he had surrendered to a sixteen-year-old girl!

You're a soldier on a battlefield, armored up and ready
to fight. The trumpets sound the call to engage, and you
move forward with your brigade. The two armies clash.
You notice that your companions to the right and left of
you go down, and then you take a sword to the shoulder.
Looking up, you expect to see a mustachioed Frenchman
trampling over you, but instead you see a young woman
giving a battle cry for her troops to continue moving forward. In your dying breaths, the world as you knew it
and as you expected it to function has radically changed:
French, peasant teenagers, after all, don't kill professional
English soldiers.

Through experience and common sense, we build up
for ourselves interpretations of how the world works and
what we can expect from it. We plan our lives based on
these interpretations, defining for ourselves, our families,
and our communities how we'll act within the world. We
believe that we've got the world figured out and even try
to selfishly conform the world to our desires. Then something breaks into this interpretation of the world and
radically alters it. The world simply didn't function as we
expected it to function.

Joan of Arc-God represents hermeneutic theology's concept. She will not meet your expectations; she'll defy them.

As a God-concept, Joan of Arc is not identity as such;
not pure will, nor a being among other beings—be that
being hippie or retired. Joan of Arc *is* our defied expectations; she *is* this new way of experiencing the world.
Joan of Arc-God breaks open the possibilities we thought

THE ACOLYTE

Does this mean God is more of a happening than a something?

defined and circumscribed the world, defies them, and draws us into an ever-new and ever-expanding way of interpreting the cosmos. This set of possibilities includes how we understand God and ourselves as well.

Prior to Joan of Arc, the Hundred Years' War represented an upper-class fight over the French crown and whether the descendants of Edward III of England had a right to it. Joan of Arc had a series of visions that commanded her to drive the English out of France, and she saw this war as a religious war dedicated to freeing the French from illicit English rule. Much of the rest of France followed her, creating the now-adamant separation between French and English nationalities. By way of her visions, this young woman managed to swing the interpretive lens of the war: from a boring fight between dynastic heirs into a religious war to drive out the English.

Whether Joan of Arc of was correct in reinterpreting this war religiously, she creates an interesting example of the type of God at stake. Joan of Arc-God reinterprets you, and in the process reinterprets the world. This reinterpretation has two possible trajectories: the philosophical and the Christian.

The philosophical understanding of Joan of Arc-God understands her movements as being totally and completely unpredictable in her reinterpretations of our

If a hippie God that changes made you uncomfortable, Joan sounds like wishy-washy personal relativism I was warned about at Apologetics training.

THE DEACON

worlds. She stands for chaos, as there is no rationale about how she will provoke us to relate to our world's next development. From her, the only thing to expect is the unexpected, and in this way she can be similar to Jersey Shore-God. However, the Christian Joan of Arc-God is understood under the auspices of the self-sacrificial cross. She constantly calls us away from our selfish world and into a self-sacrificial world of Christian giving, a world in which we're to understand our possibilities from the ever-expanding standpoint of love.

Finally, we need to take note of a certain dilemma within the interpretive process. Socrates' friend Meno states it best:

> How will you look for it, Socrates, when you do not know at all what it is? How will you aim to search for something you do not know at all? If you should meet with it, how will you know that this is the thing you did not know?[4]

Neither the mayor of Auxerre nor the professional English soldier have any expectations that would allow them to think that their worlds have been shaken by a sixteen-year-old peasant girl. They have nothing in their experience or interpretation of the world that would even clue them in to the idea that these events were possibilities. They're in the dark about the possibility of a Joan of Arc, not only without the knowledge that she exists, but also without any expectation that she *can* exist.

So, too, on the side of God. The world itself gives us no particular reasons for buying the idea that anything like a God exists. After all, the world is chaotic and non-sensical at points, and the only ones who seem helpful are humans themselves—and we screw things up as much as save things. Moreover, we seem through the sciences and progress of technology to have gotten a stranglehold on the way the world works, able to make it submit to our wills and desires. *We* are the gods and need no other, and we most certainly can't recognize a god who doesn't fit our own controlling image.

THE BISHOP

How does this philosophical version count as a belief in God? It seems more a belief in the human origin of what we label God.

For these reasons, Joan of Arc-God depends on the idea of self-revelation. For the world to know God, God must reveal herself as Joan of Arc and as these defied expectations. Without Joan of Arc lifting the facemask on her helmet, neither the mayor nor the soldier would have any idea of just who hit them. Joan of Arc must show herself in order to be seen as Joan of Arc. In this way, she is a self-revealing God, known no other way than through her own self-revelation, which is found for Christian interpreters solely on the divinely made sense of the cross.

Again, this notion of self-revelation has both a philosophical and theological option. Philosophically, this self-revelation is a revelation of chaos. God is the act of what philosophers have come to call *deconstruction*, which refers to that experience of when our worlds and expectations fall apart before our eyes. My move from a tit-for-tat God to the God of philosophy was, for instance, grounded in an act of deconstruction in that the logic of what I held dear fell crumbled, opening me to broader interpretations. From the philosophical Joan of Arc-God, I experienced God's self-revelatory deconstruction of my world, and I should likely expect it again.

Theologically, things are more complicated. To recall the initial scriptures cited, Joan of Arc-God is a self-revelation of our defied expectations, but she is this self-revelation under the contrary expectations of the cross (or what Luther calls *sub contrario*). According to traditional, Miyagi-based, theological wisdom, God is not related to us—God is Other. God should not be found to care for us much less die for us. But that is who we find God to be on the cross: the one who defies our expectations not neutrally, as in the philosophical interpretation, but out of love. God defies our expectations because God is unwilling to leave us to our own nonloving devices.

Joan of Arc-God is the self-revelatory experience with defied expectations. For a long time, I've taught, written, and thought because, ya know, I'm a philosopher and theologian. I consider this work ministerial in its own right, and I believe I serve my God and church through it. Nonetheless, I've recently been put in charge of a ministry program within the theology major at my school. I'm not talking the kind of ministry I thought I was doing, either, a vague and indirect form of thinking about God and relaying such thoughts to students. I've now got under my care students who want to work with teenagers—as in fourteen-, fifteen-, and sixteen-year-olds, whom I know as much about as a fish does about rocket science!

Truthfully, as an academic, I expected to drink a lot of tea, write a lot of heady books, and give a lot of wordy lectures about stuff like ontology and hermeneutics, but now I'm helping train ministers for my diocese and beyond. This experience of defied expectations is, I believe, an experience with Joan of Arc-God. She has shown me something about myself and my world that I didn't know and

---

THE BISHOP

Hopefully you won't have St. Augustine's experience and end up getting shoehorned into being a bishop. I don't think bishops get to write like this. ;)

---

wouldn't have expected to know, and she's beckoned me to a different world beyond the safe one I had built for myself.

Joan of Arc-God emerged in twentieth-century Germany from Lutheran philosophical theologians such as Eberhard Jüngel, Gerhard Ebeling, and Ingolf Dalferth. Both

Dalferth and Jüngel depend somewhat on Jersey Shore-God as a starting point, but they fix his problems by putting him through rehab. Jüngel denies that there exists an absolute hiddenness in God that's separable from the love of God as found on the cross, which Luther always worried about. Love exhausts God, even if we don't know the full extent of the love that comes to us ever anew. Joan of Arc also has some sway on U.S. thinkers such as John D. Caputo, who reasons to her by way of Jacques Derrida and generally upholds the philosophical view that God is the act of deconstruction— God is the act of cracking open cultural ways of interpreting things in order to show their human fragility.

Would you call this Joan of Arc-God a Creator? Does She create and crack all things? Geez! She is almost as frustrating her namesake killing in the name of God.

THE ELDER

Any which way you take Joan of Arc-God, she shares a certain defiance through all her varieties. She reveals herself and then defies all our expectations, not only with how to understand the world and ourselves, but also with our understandings of her. She is your experience of the world and the expectation that the world as it stands need not imply that it must remain this way. Joan of Arc constantly and consummately calls you back to the unexpected. In its best forms, I believe that the unexpected emerges through an ever-expanding selfless and spontaneous love, and we come to experience this love through the worldly habits we confront and overcome through her.

Conclusion

Both Hippie Aunt-God and Joan of Arc-God give us a lot of new theological fodder. Both of them have emerged at a time when the scientific revolution has been better understood, and so they might better be able to stand up to the test of reason as aligned with the demands of modern thought. Both of them have a real existential and relational sense to them so that it doesn't feel like we're simply thinking about God without relating to God. And, no doubt, both concepts have been a boon to contemporary forms of spirituality, especially those that would seek to quell an overestimation of the human-centeredness of earlier versions of God. These concepts aren't going away any time soon.

That said, an important task remains. We've talked concepts, but now we need to talk truth, namely: Which of these concepts holds the best possibility for becoming our conception of God and which other concepts may become supplementally important? We need to ask whether God-concepts, like car engines, were really built better in the old days when artisans took pride in their craft, or whether we get something better today with the advent of modern technology? To this set of questions, we need to turn.

Sifting the Beer
from the Suds

After all this talk of God-concepts, I need a beer. Although we may find it difficult to think about God in ways other than what we already culturally believe, once we try it on for size, we see that it's productive. It brings freedom and understanding to our lives and worlds. For instance, we have a new apparatus to distinguish between bad sermons and good sermons; does the preacher advocate for Jersey Shore-God, Joan of Arc-God, or something else? If it's Jersey Shore, we might rightfully decide to space off. We also have a way to begin questioning our interpretations of the Bible: Can God actually get angry, or is God an eternally stable point? Most importantly, we have a way to think through our cultural overestimation of our commonsense understandings of these ideas of God in the first place: that God is a cosmic vending machine in the form of a shredded old man.

Speaking of beer, we need to sift the beer from the suds of the IPA of God-concepts we just cracked open. We need to try to make sense out of what is true and what is false in our developed conceptions of God. To this end, I'll drop two of our grumpier grandparents off at home for a nap: Jersey Shore- and Retired Oprah-Gods. Respectively, Hippie Aunt- and Joan of Arc-Gods give us the benefits of each of the previous gods without all of the uncomfortably racist war stories. After all, Hippie Aunt-God is similar to deism in that she's a being among other beings, but she's better than Oprah because she actually relates to her beings through her cosmic drum circle. Moreover, Joan of Arc-God draws out the idea of self-revelation that Luther's Jersey Shore-God so heavily depends on without the potential of her drunkenly flashing you.

THE ACOLYTE

I think your new pantheon needs a children's cartoon. Something like the Superfriends meets the Highlander.

I begin, though, with the only place to begin: Miyagi!

The Ontological Primacy of Mr. Miyagi

Remember how Miyagi is an unathletic-looking old man? The rest of these concepts certainly remember this fact, and they generally stand around the pantheon making fun of him. He's "out of date," "slow," "static," "can't account for evolution," "can't relate to the new generations," or "lacks power to get anything done." Miyagi-God is also a karate master, which is why he just totally blocked every attack thrown his way.

You see, Miyagi-God is impenetrable in a certain respect. He stands as the identity underlying all other God definitions. Because he *is* identity—he's also the highest concept—all other understandings of God will invoke his existence indirectly and have every insult, punch, or take-down thrown at him reversed. Calling God an absolute will (Jersey Shore), in process (your Hippie Aunt), the highest being (Oprah), or even an experience with the world (Joan of Arc) already depends on *identity* to make sense of these terms.

I think this is something that made sense to me the day after my intro to philosophy class in undergrad . . .

THE BISHOP

For instance, Hippie Aunt-God famously criticizes Miyagi-God for emphasizing the reality of being over becoming because Miyagi is an unchanging ground of order rather than changing with the emerging and evolving world order. She's correct in her accusation, as Miyagi-God does emphasize absolute identity and stability, but she's wrong in thinking reality could do without this recognition. After all, Hippie Aunt-God sees that at least some principles of thought cannot change lest the reality of change changes itself, but this has been Miyagi God's point all along.[1] So long as Hippie Aunt-God recognizes that something in this world cannot change, she recognizes that all reality itself depends on an ultimate constancy, a stability point that absolutely remains separable from the highest reality. In fact, Hippie Aunt-God's identity itself depends on Miyagi-God in that without any such stability point, you couldn't recognize Hippie Aunt-God.

The same counterargument could be made in reference to any of the other God-concepts. Each of their

THE DEACON

Isn't this why
Whitehead differentiates
God from Creativity?
#HippieAuntWasWhispering

identities actually depends on affirming the prior reality of Miyagi-God. Without the stability that emerges from Miyagi-God, there can be no identity whatsoever.

Let me get super theologically and Catholically nerdy on you for a moment about this argument. We Catholics have a theologian that we call *the* Theologian, which makes for one heck of a monk's cassock to fill given the length of the Catholic tradition and the number of theologian-monks in it. To be honest, this rather girthy theologian was known to fill out cassocks quite well and the pages of books even better. I'm talking about Thomas

Aquinas, the Dumb Ox, and we all need to drink a little of his thought straight from the source.[2] Allow me this one quote where this divulger of theological coolness famously proclaims: "God is his own knowing. . . . Our knowing signifies awareness as though it were a quality of things whereas in God it is his very substance; and knowledge names a disposition not always acknowledged in man, whereas in God it is pure activity."[3]

To those uninitiated in the throes of Thomas-talk, allow me to reinterpret. God is not some being external to

---

Dumb Ox it is! Now
tell Balaam something.
#BibleNerdJoke

THE ACOLYTE

---

us who knows things external to God. That's how every other school of interpreting God envisions their God with the exception of the hermeneutic: as some being separable from its act of knowing. For Aquinas, God is the light of intellect itself; the very act of knowing who knows any and all other things, not externally as do we finite, material-based knowers, but internally, as the one who illumines and shines order on all things as their ordering-point. There simply is no knowing, finite or infinite, without the infinite light of Intellect itself, who's absolutely inseparable from its extant being and all other beings. We can't talk any of the other concepts of God without such an act of being and intellect because talk of any other concept depends on this light of God's being. To try to make other god-concepts into God we must do so while rejecting the ability to think at all. Such is Miyagi.

The second problem we run into with Miyagi comes from a very serious but ultimately ill-founded objection: injustices done in the name of Miyagi. Persons often note that this vision of God as the supreme reality whose perfection disallows him a sense of change makes for an interpretation of God as distant, unsympathetic, and even tyrannical toward us. To be honest, the tyranny claim is merely a mistaken attribution of the characteristics of Jersey Shore and its sense of omnipotence to Miyagi, so we can reject that one almost handily. Still, the others ring true, and I have some sympathy toward their tone.

Still, as I've gotten a bit older, I've come to find out that my father was often emotionally and intellectually acerbic to other people. He wasn't intentionally mean, but he was insensitive and failed in many ways to empathize with, hear out, or take others seriously. My dad was also, fortunately, gregarious and funny, so I doubt that he's remembered by most folks in solely the above, gruff manner, save for a few people. I say all these things from second-hand memories: through people who've told me some stories about my dad that disturbed me a bit. I simply didn't know him in this context; he was never gruff, short, or in any way contemptuous with me. Sure, he'd push me to work harder as any good parent does, but he always showed a deep sensitivity to me and a love that perhaps few other people knew through him.

Miyagi has been accused by contemporary critics of being the interpretive cause of any number of oppressions, including empire-building, wage-withholding, slavery-owning injustices. And, no doubt, these critics can be right: people have done precisely such stupid things in the name of God. Some of the first images of Constantine, the first Roman emperor to go Christian, directly reflected this idea. As God was the head of heaven, so Constantine was the ruler of earth, meaning all others were his subjects.

For these reasons, many critics advocate a social-justice oriented rejection of Miyagi for more sympathetic concepts, especially Hippie Aunt. While the issue is real

I think I might have an inner hippie under my vestments.

THE BISHOP

enough, I simply want to point out that we often fail to notice that people generally do crappy things in the name of *anything* and not merely Miyagi, Jersey Shore, or anyone else from our grandparents' pantheon. Hell, any concept can serve as an interpretive excuse for oppression and not merely Miyagi. For instance, I believe that Hippie Aunt doesn't discipline this creation well enough, so I'll seek to discipline it myself by building massive cities to ward off any possibility of interacting with an unhinged nature and beat it back into submission. I'm jesting with this idea, but I'm dead serious when I say that we persons can turn *anything* into an excuse to oppress folks. We need not to take oppression merely as some kind of intellectual

THE DEACON

Since humans can use anything to oppress, why isn't that a design flaw for Miyagi?

ideology arising solely from some concepts and not from others but a disease of our wills. In this way, even Jersey Shore can potentially be applied in good ways as well as negative, which is the only light I've shined on the concept for very specific purposes.

Whatever reactions you have to Miyagi-God, the whole picture simply can't be reduced to the idea that this concept somehow oppresses. Any truth can be oppressive or freeing, can be used as a cattle-prod or the key to our mind's gate, and an understanding of God can yield a curt and off-putting side or a sensitive and loving side. This idea is true of Miyagi as well. In fact, as I came to grips with Miyagi-God through my B.A. and M.A. studies, I always saw Miyagi as the ground of Goodness that allowed me to interact with all things peacefully, lovingly, and with a sense of relational respect. Just like my father, Miyagi never showed me these other possibilities except through external critics.

A Drunken Miyagi

Still, Miyagi-God's opponents are correct to note some important vulnerabilities. The greatest vulnerability with Miyagi-God is that he really doesn't matter in an existential sense. Miyagi-God does very little for us on an everyday level. A famous critique from a philosopher named Martin Heidegger simply claims that no one's inspired to worship Miyagi-God. After all, as philoso-

---

Wouldn't the opposite be true?

THE ACOLYTE

---

phers have historically conceived him, the highest reality doesn't *need* any reality lower than himself. To need anything other than oneself is imperfection, and Miyagi-God is, as the highest reality, impenetrably perfect. So Miyagi-God remains at home, at peace, and content simply thinking through just how freaking awesome he is in the same way I imagine Bruce Wayne must do about being Batman.

As unflinching as Miyagi-God seems, he also has a softer side. In a touching scene in *The Karate Kid*, Mr. Miyagi gets drunk, sings, and cries over his lost wife. So, too, with Miyagi-God: in a state of cosmic drunkenness that will only be meted out by Jesus's wine-producing miracle at Cana, you can get him thinking relationally, and that's very important. If we are to conceive of Miyagi-God as having any value beyond the intellectual, he'll eventually have to reach out to us and relate to the world in such a way that he makes a difference. Leaving open the question for now as to *whether* Miyagi-God actually relates to the world in any such manner, we can hypothetically explore *how* God might engage in a relation, and that makes room for some of the interesting components to emerge from both Hippie Aunt-God and Joan of Arc-God.

THE ELDER

Why wouldn't a Christian theologian start with God-with-us in Christ and then work toward God's perfect divine intellect?

Hippie Aunt-God's drum circle can become a bit, shall we say, awkward. But you can't argue with her about one thing: you always have a good time. You can see an intrinsic beauty amidst the pulsating rhythms coming from so many different people, even if the bulk are from the same, '60s, white, protest demographic. We need to more adequately express the truth of this drum circle, then, because it does create a beautifully interwoven relationship between God and the world.

The benefit of this god-concept stems from its dynamic lens. Proponents of Hippie Aunt-God conceive of her as existing in time and in a constant state of relational becoming with her creation. She takes the world into herself in each moment of the world's existence, calls it to its best possible way of becoming, and then gives herself back over to the world as the power to pursue its best possibilities, changing right alongside with it. She gives us a way of conceiving how an otherwise distant God such as Miyagi-God potentially relates to our world. The question is how to incorporate this vision into Miyagi-God.

We need only to take an idea already at play within Miyagi-God and reinterpret it to do so. The idea of Miyagi-God is that he is the identity that undergirds the world. Metaphorically, this idea portrays Miyagi-God as the primary rhythm-keeper in the drum circle of this world, the main source of this world's harmonic life. In other words, Miyagi-God is the drum leader to which all other players within the circle respond, only Miyagi-God's rhythm remains constant, unperturbed, and steady. His rhythm gives all other players the room and space they need in order to play their own beautiful solos in accordance with their own peculiar natures.

What I'm saying is that Miyagi-God can potentially exist in a state of constant relationality with the world, and Hippie Aunt gives us the tools to think this possibility through. As grounding all identity within the world, this God need not be distant from it, even if he is often mistakenly thought of that way. Rather, God is already deeply connected to the world and, like Hippie Aunt-God, *can* potentially call the world from within the world to its best possibilities in each and every moment that it changes, if this god cares to do so. Certainly, in such a vision, advocates of Hippie Aunt lose the sense of God changing *with* the world, but I'm not sure that's an entirely huge loss, not if relationality rather than change remains the important characteristic from the Hippie Aunt-God perspective.

After all, if I express to my mother that I hate her, and I surely did just that as a teenager, I wouldn't want her to express this same hate back, changing her stance on love for me. Only a bad parent would do that. Hippie Aunt-God has the potential, it seems, for precisely this kind of change if, for some reason, her activity of changing becomes the most important aspect of her identity rather than her capacity to personally relate to us. If we take Hippie Aunt's relationality while rejecting something like her

THE DEACON

Whitehead argues that while God changes in relationship to each moment, God's character never changes. God's greatest limitation is God's infinite, unwavering love. #PrimordialNature

attitude toward us changing, she actually accords with and describes well the stated relational possibility within Miyagi-God: that God can relate to us by calling us to our best possibilities without withholding his love if we should fail to live up to our potential. I'm good with that.

Miyagi Gets a Transplant

The second way in which Miyagi-God can become more relatable is by having something like an experience with him, whatever that word might mean. I defer to Hollywood for help, and not in the money-generating manner that the previous two clauses seem to imply. No butt-shots in this book. In what was surely the nadir of their careers, Nicolas Cage and John Travolta starred in an awesome '90s action movie called *Faceoff*. The movie tells the story about how an FBI agent (Travolta) gets a face transplant to make him look like a terrorist he wants to catch (Cage). The terrorist does the same. I have no memory of the rest of the plot, and who cares! All that matters are the awesome action antics ensued.

Here's the point: Miyagi-God needs a face transplant. As a God-concept, people have a difficult time relating to him in their experience, but Joan of Arc-God gives us something to latch onto within our experience, albeit not directly in the way we experience, for instance, a delicious pizza. She is, rather, a self-revelation of defied expectations, the one who pops up and transforms our understanding of moments from what we think they should be to what they really are.

Relating this idea to Miyagi-God can be tough. More than even process thinkers, hermeneutic theologians believe that Miyagi-God is nonsense. But, again, I'm not entirely sure how you can get rid of this God and still talk with a sense of truth given Miyagi-God's relationship to identity, which is why I don't buy the hermeneutic position in its fullness. I still believe that these two ideas converge and can commingle at the level of what classical theists call God's incomprehensibility.

Incomprehensibility means that Miyagi-God is so rad and has such a cool Harley that you can't come close to grasping who he is in his fullness. This inability doesn't mean that God can't be grasped in principle—as the most basic concept, Miyagi-God is the most knowable reality in all the cosmos. We finite persons just don't have the mental tools to know God in his full knowability, which is why Thomas Aquinas imagines in a way only possible for

THE ELDER

> Only theologians make
> commingling around
> incomprehensibility
> a job!

a philosopher-monk that heaven means standing around doing new syllogisms about God and trying to know cumulatively more about the One who is infinitely knowable. Infinity's a long time to write syllogisms, which I'll only assent to because it sounds only *slightly* better than the vision some of your religious leaders may have given you: that heaven is something like a church service where we stand around singing praises of God's glory eternally. Eternity's a long time to fake like I'm praying.

I digress.

With this notion in mind, and with the hypothetical possibility that God actually relates to us through the work of the drum circle, I believe that we'd be well within our rights to claim that God acts out this relationship by defying our expectations in an act of self-revelation. I mean, we all reach points in our lives in which we think that we know exactly who we are and who God is. These points close us off, giving us over to creature comforts and easy habits. We lose sight of the fact that this world is not for our consumption and that God's not our errand boy, delivering the world over to us as we desire it. God is incomprehensible, infinite, and self-revelatory, in defiance of our expectations, which we come to know in these special moments of interruption.

Karl Barth said, "It may be that when the angels go about their task praising God, they play

THE BISHOP

only Bach. I am sure, however, that when they are together with one's family they play Mozart." I am optimistic that come 5 p.m. on Friday they all play Willie Nelson's "Whiskey River" with their friends.

So if we transplant Joan of Arc-God's surprisingly teenage face onto Miyagi-God's incomprehensible head, we get a God who not only leads the world in a cosmic drum circle but a God who shows up in our everyday lives, too. Miyagi-God (with a face transplant) is the one who defines our experience of the world in love, and defies our expectations of what that could mean and be. Miyagi-God comes to us and calls us out of our worldly possibilities and into the possibility of divine love.

I think I want this on a T-shirt. Then I could use it at confirmation camp!

THE DEACON

God's a French Hippie Karate-Master, and Not a Cosmic Vending Machine

We now need to make a switch. In the previous chapter, I spoke about the image of God we all tend to have, a muscular Old-Man River, one to whom we can make certain magical incantations in order to receive whatever we're asking for. I propose that we switch this image of God with Miyagi, with the face of Joan of Arc, and leading a drum circle: a mash-up of God concepts in the name of relationality and on the grounds of incomprehensibility. We can't do away with Miyagi-God because all talk whatsoever depends on his existence. Still, Miyagi-God is pulled out of himself into potential relationship with the world by Hippie Aunt-God, and that relationship looks a lot like God defying our expectations of what we want to the world to be: comfortable for us.

No, God's definition has nothing to do with a cosmic vending machine but with the melding of these above ideas. This book begins with the philosophy of God, but it will move decidedly toward a theology of the cross. If you remember your literature well enough, you'll note that Jesus is the most famous historical example for us of someone hung on a Roman cross, and Jesus is found in the Bible, which may surprise you, I know. I point these items out because I've said from the beginning that the Catholic worldview has to accept both the philosopher's God and the biblical God—the God of reason and the God of relation. While Miyagi works perfectly well in a philosophical context, he won't be able to do full justice to Christian theology and its biblical underpinnings, not without incorporating these important ideas from Hippie Aunt and Joan of Arc.

If God is one who saves, God must be able to draw out of us our best, most unselfish possibilities, which means God must relate to us. So while God's primary philosophical meaning has to do with the identity undergirding all things in the world, God's biblical identity pertains to relating to this world and calling it back to the divinely pulsating melody not merely its own. The incomprehensible God is one who actively beckons this world, one who calls us to reject the disharmonies within the world as we've become familiar and even enhance, and stand once more in cosmic solidarity with both God and all of creation as God shines light on these things anew. That starts with the concept of Miyagi but doesn't end with him.

Is God Spiritual but Not Religious?

Having developed five concepts of God and the truth of their relationships to one another, we need to ask: Can we actually know or develop any such concepts with something like an idea of truth in mind at all? I pose this question because it seems so massively arrogant to think that we—a group of small, furless animals on the planet Earth—could say anything true about the creator of the universe. Most certainly a God, if any such God even exists, stands above our feeble ways of talking. At best, God chuckles at our attempts to make sense of the divine being. At worst, we're being completely ignored.

I think this feeling was at the bottom of my student's thoughts when, in a comparative religion course, as we were talking about why folks were interested in the class to begin with, she said, "I want to take the class because, you know, I'm 'down' with religion but I'm not *'down-down'* with religion. I just want to meditate." I get it; sometimes religion and the talk that comes from it feel forced, false, lacking any meaning. That's why in the next

---

THE ACOLYTE

I can understand not wanting to double-down on religion!

---

two chapters, we're setting the direct concept of God to the side for a bit and dealing with a correlate idea: our God-talk in and through religious traditions.

We have to ask ourselves what it means to talk about God through religion, whether such talk has any meaning to it given God's status as most rad, and whether or not religions get anything right in their talk about God. Accordingly, we need to think extensively about the question of the relationship of God to our traditional talk of God. We'll begin thinking through what's become an important terminology today: being spiritual but not religious. We need to figure out what this terminology means, what it questions, and where it may be useful or, as I'll argue, not so useful.

Bourbon Tasting

In 2013, my wife and I were living in Southern Maryland, the most humid and mosquito-ridden place you can imagine. We needed a break from both. After the school where I was teaching had gotten out for the year, we went to

Louisville, where my wife has family. We also got tickets to the Kentucky Derby. The time we spent there solidified two things for me: first, as a born-and-bred Westerner, I will never understand the world of high-end horse racing; and second, bourbon is the world's finest spirit.

While in Kentucky, we went bourbon tasting on what's unsurprisingly called the Bourbon Trail. We had a blast but didn't get blasted. In fact, one of the pesky things about bourbon tasting at a distillery comes from all the

---

That's the type of trail that makes me want to go hiking.

THE ELDER

---

decorum. They *unbelievably* make you drink out of sipping glasses instead of, say, massive goblets. And they only give you around half-an-ounce of bourbon per pour, or whatever's deemed appropriate by state liquor licensing laws. Both the glass and the amount tend to get in the way of what you and I really want to do at the distillery: give all the bourbons a quick try and then stick a straw in your favorite bourbon barrel for a long draught.

We oftentimes feel something similar when it comes to the relationship between religion and spirituality. We want to try, test, and sip many varieties, and we want to drink deeply from several of them, but there are pesky rules about religious commitments and tradition. Religions don't tend to let you sample their wares—they want a full commitment from you. If you're going to be Muslim, you've got to pray five times per day and fast during

Ramadan; if you're going to be Buddhist, you've got to meditate and follow the Noble Eightfold Path. Because of the significant commitment that religions demand, we've created *spiritual but not religious*. It's the equivalent of sipping a bunch of different bourbons without ever buying a bottle. It's being a taster.

THE BISHOP

It's a bit hazy in my memory, but in college I learned that overtasting a multiplicity of adult beverages can double-down the hangover.

Tasters usually claim that they don't buy into this human-made bunk and that, instead, they buy into something more primordial, beautiful, and ethereal—something that was here *before* we started mucking everything up with religious doctrine and belief. Or else, frankly, they just want an excuse to claim that yoga class can substitute for church.

I'm drawn here to a *very* important article from the farcical newspaper, *The Onion*. The article, "Priest Religious but Not Really Spiritual," goes like this:

> BOSTON—Father Clancy Donahue of St. Michael Catholic Church told reporters Wednesday that while he believed in blindly adhering to the dogma and ceremonies of his faith, he tried not to get too bogged down by actual spirituality. "I'm not so much into having a relationship with God as I am into mechanically conducting various rituals," Donahue said. "To me, it just feels

empty to contemplate a higher power without blindly obeying canon law and protecting the church as an institution." Donahue emphasized that although he did not personally agree with those who pondered the eternal, he had nothing against them.[1]

I'm utterly taken by how well this fake and hilarious article captures the phenomenon of being spiritual-but-not-religious and what it seeks to avoid: empty ritualism, legalism, and a stark advocacy of tradition on the mere grounds of "what we've always done, we should always do." That is, the goal of bourbon tasters is to get beyond the many human rules and get a taste of the divine directly, regardless of what socially constructed religions have to say about the subject.

For these reasons, we live increasingly in a world of religion-tasters: persons who intentionally identify with being spiritual but not religious. While the above rejection of rule-oriented legalism is a very good thing, this religion-tasting world as a whole is a mixed bag. The good news is that persons of such a variety aren't usually as overly zealous as their explicitly religious counterparts, unless we count Twitter activism as zealous. I fear, however, that such folks have lost sight of the real, important, and undeniable role of tradition in their lives, which is a shame for a number of important reasons.

Swimming in Bourbon

Allow me one completely uninteresting bourbon fact to begin explaining mysticism. Bourbon distilleries age their bourbons in a warehouse—often called a *rickhouse*.

I specifically remember walking into one distillery on my tasting journey and being amazed by the number of barrels shelved throughout the warehouse. Each barrel holds about fifty-three gallons, and a thought crossed my mind: What if some sneaky employee got into the bourbon warehouse at night and popped the caps off of all the barrels? How deep would that employee be wading in bourbon if the warehouse flooded? My uneducated guess was that the resulting flood of bourbon would come up to the employee's waist—enough to go swimming in but not enough to drown. I also solemnly believe that such an event would fulfill Amos's prophetic vision that the mountains would drip and flow with bourbon (also translated as "wine" in lesser editions of the Bible).[2] As with this flood of bourbon, so too with God-experiences for a mystic.

The mystic seems to be the original claimant to the title of taster, managing to do so without even wearing today's customary yoga pants. Mystics leave behind the confines of human language and engage the being of God directly through "mystical experiences." These experiences can take on any number of forms.

THE ACOLYTE

In my experience you shouldn't listen to a spiritual guide wearing Lululemon. Why? Because you can see right through them.

Some mystics describe themselves as being taken up into an unending bliss, which makes sense. God, after all, is the goal of all things, that which we desire in itself, so any direct experience with God would mean a total satiation of our other desires. Then again, some mystics describe the deep sorrow of seeing their true self within a context of divine luminosity. Again, this idea makes sense as it's kind of like seeing what a bar floor looks like when the lights come up: you didn't know how many dirty old pork rinds were either on the ground or in your soul prior to this divine unveiling. Others even express certain sexual satisfaction within the divine being, God being the one who can infinitely fulfill and redefine any desire, even sexual desire, that you may have.

Heck, Thomas Aquinas had a mystical experience with God just prior to his death. He went on to claim that the whole of his work was mere chaff! That's a strong statement from one who can discuss the intricacies of the Trinity better than you or I can talk about a basic Sloppy Joes recipe. Any way you look at it, mystics *seem* to swim in the flooded warehouse of bourbon unhindered by the

---

Was Miyagi-God disappointed in Ol' Tom?

THE ELDER

---

barrels of human language, taking the immediate experience of the divine flood of bourbon and trying to put that experience into a set of words that extend beyond their normal usage.

This fact also confirms a second point. Mystics do generally sound drunk when you try to read them.

Most mystics seem to express the being and nature of God almost a-religiously, without any reference to doctrine, dogma, or human thought. Within the inner being of God, all things are united in a blissful experience of the divine and, in this way, it seems that mystics confirm what we already thought we knew: that human language cannot capture God's spiritual-but-not-religious being.

THE DEACON

The mystics' lack of clarity, erotic language for God, and invitations to silent prayer were all my youth minister needed to spot satan sneaking into the church through centering prayer.

As persons more comfortable with bourbon tasting, we may think that we should emulate these mystics at first. After all, we need to find our way beyond the human-made barrels of God-talk stored up in our traditional mental warehouses and allow instead the divine to flood us with the sweet nectar of God's bourbony being. We need to ignore all the ways in which we try to limit God and instead let God explode Godself into our lives without any pre-formed thoughts. In fact, one reason we respond well to the idea of becoming a taster stems from a belief that God *as* God cannot be contained by our thought. It seems, in fact, that were God to be contained by our thought, the God we're claiming to think about would be no God at all. God, too, is spiritual but not religious, free from the trappings of human-made thought and its social inculcation.

I think half of my congregation would agree with this. The same ones that get uncomfortable NOT adding a word between Jesus Christ.

THE BISHOP

So we feel the need to sneak into our own mental warehouses, and we begin to uncork all the thoughts we have about God. We flood the warehouses of our minds with bourbon and allow the unhinged thoughts to work through our neural pathways, just as God remains unhinged. As good as that sounds in theory, I have serious reservations regarding how far we can go with this type of experience and rejection of human language, especially when we begin thinking that the experiences are totally delinked from tradition that emerges in and through our forms of talking.

Aged Bourbon, New Bourbon-Skins

We can talk about the many positive benefits of mystics, and especially those like Meister Eckhart and Teresa of Avila, both of whom are revered today. They deserve their place in the annals of religious creativity, for they force us to think beyond our usual boundaries. They ask us to give up the dogmatisms that we hold onto simply because, frankly, we fear the uncomfortable truths beyond them. That's the real innovation of the mystic: they challenge our usual assumptions about God and the ways in which we're comfortable talking about God. That's also why descriptions of God in terms of satisfying sexual desires, for instance, can be so helpful. Mechthild of Magdeburg, which in fact *is not* a proto-Steampunk name for a new *Bioshock* sequel, writes,

> Lord, now I am a naked soul
> And you in yourself All-Glorious God.
> Our mutual intercourse
> Is eternal life without end.[3]

In this passage, we're forced into honesty: to look at ourselves as the sexual, desire-driven beings that we are, and then see that any and all of these desires take their ultimate reference from the divine. That's not icky; that's beautiful!

Still, we can push the mystical point too far. For one, most of us are not mystics, and so we're stuck with the mental apparatuses that we've got when we think about God. Though we may revere certain mystics, we cannot depend on the authority of their experiences to discuss God. We still need to learn to speak for ourselves. Further, even mystics are bound to human-made traditions and language, a point that we certainly need to sip on for a bit longer.

Before taking my distillery tours, I just assumed that the mash from which the bourbon is distilled created most of the flavor in the finished product. But in fact, much of the taste comes from the actual oak barrels in which bourbon gets aged. And a big part of this process comes from charring. Before aging a bourbon, the inside of the barrel is burned, and different depths of char will produce different tastes to the bourbon. The deeper and longer the char, the more sugars (and carcinogens) will be released into the bourbon.

After charring the barrel, the mash product—what's essentially moonshine—is aged in the barrel. In this stage, temperature is the main flavor-producing mechanism because it causes the barrel to expand and contract. Rick-houses in Kentucky are not climate controlled, and the temperature fluctuates. Barrels are rolled around over the time of their aging, picking up the varied temperature in different parts of the rickhouse, and the bourbon works its way in and out of the charred walls, bringing the sugary, oaky flavor with it back into the mash. After eight or ten or twelve years, you have the drink of the divine!

Prior to my visit to the Bourbon Trail, I didn't comprehend the importance of the barrel to the bourbon-making process in the same way that many of us fail to comprehend the importance of tradition to the process of conceiving and thinking about God. All God-concepts get thoroughly aged and defined by the religious barrels in which they're brought up.

For example, in the West, mystics tend to contemplate God's *incomprehensibility*, a concept I earlier used to talk of Miyagi. In principle, that means that *we* can know very little certain about God even if Miyagi-God remains *supremely* knowable in himself. Incomprehensibility refers to our inability to comprehend that which is inherently comprehensible in its fullness. After all, God is that iden-tity-giving point that lets us know and measure everything else. The only reason we as humans can't know God stems from the fact that we have finite intellects and therefore cannot grasp an infinite Miyagi-God. Mystics understand this point. In fact, they depend on this point as it allows them the space to be taken up by the divine in an act of giving. Mystics don't claim to put themselves into the inner life of God. In an act of grace-filled love, mystics remind us that, when it happens, God draws them into God's self and grants them a vision of the divine being.

THE BISHOP

I think the mystics direct us to the treasure in tradition, not an escape route.

I cannot emphasize this point enough. You may have noticed, for instance, lots of Instagram posts by your spiritual friends quoting Meister Eckhart, the great German mystic whose popularity has surged in the modern academy and Twittersphere alike. Postmodern philosophers—even atheist ones!—have rediscovered mystics like Eckhart, using them as blank slates onto which to project either their spiritual dreams or prophetic proclamations of nothingness. For them, all discussions of divine mystery act as a deconstructive tool for our God-talk, allowing us to say about our religiosity, "That's neat, but no thanks!" But Meister Eckhart didn't have mystical visions in a crystal-lit, cosmic cave, complete with a meditating Buddha, floating Jesus, and cross-legged Vishnu. The dude was as Catholic as could be, taking confession and serving

Eucharist each and every day. He was only taken up into mystical vision by the divine somewhere in between the many devout acts of a highly religious life. Then again, perhaps I lack the hubris to tell Meister Eckhart that what he was really doing was deconstructing Christendom and its secret propensity for a will-to-power.

Mystics, far from moving beyond tradition, push tradition to its limits. They see into the tradition in the most enviable and helpful of ways. Mystics embody tradition in its fullness and push the tradition to evolve with the God who calls it, but they do not reject it. They are very spiritual but far from a-religious, and they may have something to teach us about how to embrace both spirituality and religiosity at one and the same time.

Be the Bourbon

Mystics can't beat tradition. They don't function merely as tasters, or even apparently as swimmers. Their very experience of God depends on tradition, and that turns out to be a good thing, for tradition provides us the vocabulary to find the truth. If even mystics can't overcome tradition, we should be apt to wonder how much less we, who do not get taken up and on a ride along the cosmic skyway, should want to talk of God without tradition.

Part of the problem stems from the image we have. We think of ourselves as consumers of tradition, someone who can pop his or her head out of the liquor store of traditions, look on some finely stocked shelves, and pick up a bourbon of choice. We're tasters after all! The truth is that we've been born into a self-contradictory tradition that sees all tradition as somehow negative, which looks at

THE ACOLYTE

Is the mystical vision THE goal of tradition or an occasional perk? If it's the goal, wouldn't it relativize the tradition?

tradition with a sense of suspicion. This tradition is called the Enlightenment tradition.

Like I said, this tradition is suspicious of tradition, ignoring that its overarching suspicion might be taken up against its own suspicion. The tradition is kind of like that guy in a philosophy class who is automatically skeptical of everything the teacher and any other student has to say without ever taking the time to be suspicious of himself. We live in a tradition that allows us to think we get to choose between traditions, move in and out of traditions, reject traditions. So it has never even occurred to most people to learn to actually embrace tradition and embrace it well rather than avoid it or embrace it naïvely. Perhaps this is where the bourbon-tasting analogy breaks down. The analogy considers us as separate from the tradition that we're tasting. It takes us as outsiders looking in. In reality, we can't separate ourselves from the bourbon. We *are* the bourbon, aged and defined by our charred, oaken casks. We are our traditions, which is an idea that leads us to another important component of the bourbon-making process: the distiller.

The distillers act as quality-control checkers along each step of the bourbon-making process. The distillers know all of the proper and disgusting smells that the vats of mash should produce; they know what the liquor should taste like prior to aging; they know where to age barrels of bourbon, for how long, and what these barrels will taste like when their aging time is up.

Philosophically, we are the bourbon, but we are also the distiller, a phrase that I know makes me sound like I'm trying to be hysterically deep. I'm not; it's merely an illustration that points to the fact that we need to figure out exactly how long to age ourselves in order to make a good bottle of bourbon. If we age ourselves too long, we'll take on too much of the oak, becoming astringent. This amount of aging is tantamount to becoming a traditionalist: one who views tradition as a stopping point, a goal to be pursued for its own sake. The traditionalist misses the fact that the bourbon is not made for simply sitting in the barrel; he misses the fact that the barrel itself, while orienting toward truth, does not contain the whole of the truth.

If you are trying to convince me there is too much wood in the church it won't take much.

THE ACOLYTE

On the other hand, if we age ourselves too briefly, we'll take on too few characteristics of the oak and will be a shallow bourbon. This bourbon is the taster: the one who is spiritual but not religious. She is excited to see the world outside the bourbon barrel, to pour herself out immediately, but she's not aged properly, so she's missed out on the truth-qualities of the barrel. She therefore lacks context and vocabulary to approach a world beyond the barrel. These bourbons have no real flavor.

If we age ourselves the right amount of time, then we become the finest spirit in the world. We take on the truth-characteristics of the barrel, finding ourselves defined and oriented by these truths, only when we're poured out into a broader world, we retain these truths while opening ourselves to new, oxygenated characteristics. We stand in the truth of tradition while also opening ourselves to the beauty of the world beyond our tradition, including the God who speaks from beyond tradition. We can see the truth of tradition while refusing to reduce Truth to a formulaic version of it.

THE BISHOP

As a red wine person I hate to admit I enjoyed your bourbon metaphor.

We should strive for this third option in our God-talk. We need and depend on tradition to give us the capacity to think and talk about God, but we cannot become so reliant on tradition that we disallow God the capacity to speak for God's self.

The Master Distiller

God stands above tradition. I affirm that point wholeheartedly. God also stands within tradition, which I also affirm wholeheartedly. In fact, to say that God stands above tradition emerges as a truth found *within* tradition, so both points are necessary to affirm. Perhaps we might acknowledge these two points simultaneously by admitting yet another important bourbon-based truth: we are both the bourbon and the distiller, but we are not the master distiller.

While in Louisville, my wife's family gave me a gift bottle of bourbon signed by the master distiller of one of the famous distilleries. The bottle sits on display in our family room to this day, and for good reason. In the bourbon-making process, the master distiller stands as the ultimate developer and quality-checker. The recipe, the aging times, the final flavors all get handed down to the master distiller who has a final say over all parts of the product. We rely on the master distiller for the finished product.

We can translate this insight in a couple of important ways. For one, we can take a traditional route in the West we call talking about God by way of analogy. When we speak of God by way of analogy, we're saying that every word we use to describe God *really does* get something right about God without ever exhausting the meaning of God. For instance, when I say God is love, I admit to knowing something about what this idea means by way of my experience with love. I know that it means somehow giving of myself and receiving myself through another. When I'm in love, I cannot be who I am without another who loves me back, giving me my identity in that love. Still, I also affirm that God, as the measure and standard of anything like love, is not exhausted in my speaking of God as this love. God's being contains the full meaning and not my experience of it, so the meaning of God's love will obliterate any sense of how we can understand love, even if we really do get something of what love is in our talking about it.

THE DEACON

I think some people enjoy mystery and others use it to silence and ignore others.

Thinkers such as Augustine, Anselm, and Thomas Aquinas have taken this analogical approach for talking about God, and it's an important option because it allows us to say things about God without the seemingly obligatory, postmodern wink and nod. It's also not our only option. We can also look, for instance, for the ways that God has and continues to speak to us *within* tradition itself, and this idea makes a hermeneutic turn. After all, what we're saying now is that we can speak about God based only on how God has already spoken to us, which is to say based on God's self-revelation. Because God has spoken to us in a tradition, God continues to speak to us in and through tradition, renewing that tradition and recomposing its meaning ever anew.

We don't gain the ability to speak of God as love from nothing. This description comes from the Christian tradition, and it describes primarily what it means for God to come to us in the scandal of the cross: as self-sacrificial love. In this regard, Joan of Arc-God constantly calls us through tradition to its fullness of truth, compelling us at one and the same time not to fall into the stale barrel of traditionalism. She reinvigorates our words as Christ did Lazarus's body, and she beckons us beyond the world we think we know and into the incomprehensibility of the divine we will never know fully.

Whichever of these two paths we take, perhaps both, God is spiritual in that God both rises above, and stands inexhaustible by, tradition. Yet God is also religious in that we come to know and continue to know God through the traditions in which we develop, in which we're aged, and through which we're called. God is both spiritual and religious, and that insight portends an important secondary insight from which we can learn as well: that any real relationship with God may stem from our embracing the same characteristics and avoiding the false distinction between spirituality and religion, which usually means a naïve rejection of tradition.

6

Leave the Buddhists Alone, Already

Birth is a strange event. Yeah, yeah, yeah: it's a miracle and all that. I know that's what we're supposed to say, and I actually mostly agree. It's also just straight-up strange. I was essentially my wife's doula for our first child (which we've long-since decided was a bad idea), and I held one of her legs as she pushed the baby down the birth canal. I watched this entire event of bodily wonder happen—close up. While you might be nervous about the Hollywoodized gore of these situations at first, you get over the proliferation of bodily fluids pretty quickly both because of concern for your wife's pain and your child's health but also because the fluids are the least disconcerting thing about the birth.

Other than the straight terror of hearing my wife scream at the top of her lungs—she has since confirmed that it was the most pain she's ever been in—I couldn't stop looking at my daughter's head. As her head began to crest, I excitedly said to myself, "Wow, here she comes!" Then the head kept coming, and coming . . . and coming to the point where I started to lose focus on my skillful leg-holding and asking myself, "What the hell is wrong with my baby girl's head? Why's it so long?!" You don't realize that your newborn is going to look like a cross between E.T. and one of the characters from SNL's old "Coneheads" sketch.

THE BISHOP

Let me suggest you tell your daughter to skip this story.

I get the logic of the long head: it's gotta come out some way, and a normal-shaped head isn't going to cut the mustard, especially with the circumference of heads produced in the Halls. But then the real questions about birth, death, life, and everything in between begin to set in. You wonder who your child will be, what she'll make of herself, how she'll manage to deal with her strangely shaped head, and how you're going to screw your child up. You wonder how much you'll have influence on your child versus some natural inclinations she has, and how you can form her well. You think about questions of character, intellect, and religiosity and how you plan to raise the child. It's this last one I want to focus on.

I say birth is strange not merely because of the physical birth and all its wonderfully painful and somewhat disgusting moments, but also because birth beckons us to a certain way of existing as finite persons, ones that we'll become inculcated into. What we wear and how we eat is left completely open to chance at the time of a birth, soon to be given over to the determinations of culture, religion, and taste. This is nothing new, and it's something that each of us has likely reflected on, if only briefly: I am who I am not because of me but at least partially because of chance. I'm thrown randomly into this world, and the location of this world will determine the languages I speak and the values I uphold as true.

You at least chose to become Catholic. I discovered that was why I get to play with fire and wear these robes.

THE ACOLYTE

This chapter's about the issue of religious pluralism. In today's world, we're liable to meet any number of people who, randomly born in a different locale, are just as convinced and passionate as we are about their religious talk and beliefs, and yet they believe something totally and completely different. Because of this fact, and because of the often-beautiful ways in which people from other religions talk, we are rightly convinced that our God-talk is partly a matter of chance. I didn't have to be born in the country, culture, or language that I was, and I could've believed something totally different.

In light of this truth, we face a new dilemma, one that's become especially prevalent in the modern world. We have to ask ourselves whether God speaks to us through *one* tradition, or whether we can find something important about God from a number of traditions. That we're in one tradition rather than another, after all, seems to be a matter of chance. So we need to sort our way through the issue of religious pluralism, how we believe what we do in light of varying religious beliefs and modes of God-talk around the world, how we conceptualize and talk to others of these differing traditions, and what justifies our sticking to our own religious traditions after these talks.

One Hanks, Many Movies

A wise Westerner, drinking a latte at a local Starbucks on a Tuesday morning while pretending to write a novel, once said that "all religions are paths up the same misty mountain peak, the top of which you can't see until you get there." Then he went on to talk about "four blind men feeling a being in front of them, one of them calling it an armadillo, another a skunk, another a hose, another a tree, only to find out that, when viewed from above and as a whole, it was an elephant! They were merely feeling differing parts of it, confusing the parts for the whole. So it is with religion." Of course, you said in return, "Dude, I just want my Americano."

One option for solving the issues of religious pluralism—the wise Westerner's option and, frankly, the wrong one—is what I call the coexist option. This position, held by many proud Prius owners, is named after the second-most annoying bumper sticker in the history of this planet. (It comes only behind the NO FEAR stickers administered by men of low-esteem to their gargantuan trucks.) For the coexister, all traditions lead us to the absolutely same God, only in different ways. This needs some explanation.

What if the NO FEAR bumper sticker is printed on top of a cross?

THE DEACON

Everyone likes Tom Hanks. I'm not saying he's everyone's favorite actor (that's Denzel Washington). I'm just saying everyone enjoys at least one Hanks movie. He's starred in a bunch of interesting films: *Philadelphia*, *The Green Mile*, *Band of Brothers*, *Forrest Gump*, *You've Got Mail*, and that volleyball movie, to name just a few. At the time of this writing, he's starred in forty-three movies in thirty-five years (it'll probably be more by the time the book is printed), and those movies span every genre. He also seems like a really sweet guy.

I came to Hanks via *Forrest Gump*. While the movie's become too cliché for some, I've always found it inherently compelling, cheerily sentimental, and exuding the type of innocent loyalty and kindness I wish to see in the world. My mom's favorite Hanks movie is *You've Got Mail*.

The basic principle of our relationships to Tom Hanks is pretty simple: One Hanks, many movies. We all come to the same Hanks, but in differing ways. The coexist movement tends to emulate this Hanks-logic.

Consider the idea of *ultimate reality*. Professors use this term to refer any potential brand of divinity (or non-) from any of the religious traditions, kind of like how "facial tissue" is the generic term for what most of us call Kleenex. Ultimate reality refers to that reality, force, or energy that stands at the center of a religious tradition. It's the centerpiece toward which all the ceremonies, symbols, and ideas gain orientation. Ultimate reality is the head of a particular religious household, be that head Mom, Dad, or Moonstar.

Hanks-logic claims that everyone pursues ultimate reality, whatever its specific characteristics. We just have differing ways of getting to this same Hanks, whom we interpret through our venerated traditions. The Hindus practice *real* yoga and express their affinity for the divine through the phrase "Atman (the self) is Brahman (the source of all things)." The Buddhists pursue it through the Eightfold Path, and express it through Nirvana, which on the Christian side we awkwardly take to mean Buddhist heaven. Muslims have the Five Pillars, and find the basis of these pillars in the Qur'an. Then there are us Christians, who are generally interpreted by coexisters to have mostly oppressed and killed people.

As with Hanks, so too with God: one ultimate reality, many paths. And the coexister has answers when faced with the questions posed earlier, namely, how we believe what we do in light of varying religious beliefs and modes of God-talk around the world, how we conceptualize and talk to others of these differing traditions, and what justifies our sticking to our own religious traditions after these talks.

We believe what we do because we're finite and given over to a particular culture. We have reasonable explanations of ultimate reality based on our cultural experiences, but we have no way of prioritizing our experiences over others. Because of this situation, we move beyond any sort of actual belief in our religious tradition into a kind of dilettante belief where we think we're participating in a half-truth. Other traditions are variations on the same theme, and interreligious dialogue is a matter of broadening our view of the ultimate beyond our traditions, and making something of a synthesis of all religiosity. In turn, we find that we have no particular reason for sticking within our own belief system, other than maybe the fact that our doing so can bring a diversity of experiences to the world stage, just like our mom's kale-ginger salad brings diversity to the church picnic.

These answers are, frankly, quite good ones given their assumptions. They're just not intellectually honest, and we have to ask whether there's an alternative to Hanks-logic.

Dots and Paper

Let's imagine a sheet of paper. On that paper, someone's printed several dots, each one representing a religion. The sheet of paper itself is very important, for it forms the context in which any of these religions can show up. No paper; no dots. You can't have dots without paper.

Coexisters claim that their way of thinking represents the reality of the page itself on which many dots are printed: their position represents the ultimate reality that defines and contains all other socially constructed realities—religions—which are the dots. As the logic goes, the coexister claims to represent the illuminating context from which the real, differently interpreted but ultimately united point of any religion emerges—to illuminate and talk about the ultimate reality in the page. For the coexister, the meaning of a religion does not reside within its own tradition; the meaning comes from the page itself, which results in a generic idea of ultimate reality.

THE ACOLYTE

This is basically what I thought smart religious people thought. Good intentions. A bit boring.

The problem with this position is that, in reality, those who claim to represent the paper really form just another dot on that paper. The coexist framework doesn't provide an overall framework to understand the meaning of a plurality of religions. Or at least it doesn't form this context in any manner other than any other religious tradition can do. Christians, Hindus, Muslims, Jews—whomever. All can claim that any other religion is merely the poor-man's version of some dominant religion, which is exactly what coexisters do as well. Coexisters simply become a religion unto themselves with their own set of cultural and intellectual assumptions, and with their own set of religious symbols: bumper stickers and dream-catchers, for instance.

Second, a benign but mistaken goal overtakes coexisters. They want to ensure that peace exists among religions by showing the ways in which various faiths ultimately believe the same things. To meet this goal, coexisters gloss

Are you suggesting the coexist bumper sticker functions as a condemnation to all the religions?

THE BISHOP

over real differences in religious traditions by envisioning all these religions as dots, all about the same size and shape. (If we took a magnifying glass and looked really closely at these dots, we'd see that each dot has its own distinctive shape. I mean, *of course* Christianity is shaped like a cross; Judaism is doubtlessly shaped like the star of David; and Buddhism, the portly Indian man who founded it.) In search for some sort of sympathetic and overarching thing to say about ultimate reality, coexisters push real difference aside, and if the postmodern insights that have emerged in the past forty years have taught us *anything*, it's that we don't need to lie about or somehow cover over real differences that exist in things. By rejecting this postmodern insight, coexisters shortchange themselves by taking away the capacity to learn something real, new, and maybe even helpful from these religious traditions.[1]

Relating to other religions well doesn't mean giving in to what I'd call cafeteria religion: I pick and choose my entrees, sides, and desserts as I see fit and as I can afford them. That's the coexist trap, and it merely steals practices from a number of differing traditions, separating these practices from the goals and worldviews that allow them to make sense in the first place, generally trying to use them to get a washboard stomach. To relate to other religions well means recognizing a difficult truth: that each religion, including ours, thinks of itself as the page rather than the dots on it, and that that's okay. Let the dots be what they are and accept your undeniable role as the page because, if we can acknowledge these ideas, we can engage the various dots for what they are instead of what we want to make them. We can gain something unique, helpful, and insightful in our own pursuit, not of ultimate reality, but of God. And I can only say something about God, not as someone who is religious in general, but as a Christian.

Let's take a little journey into Buddhism as an example of how to think pluralistically in this way.

Buddhism Is Not Christianity-Lite

Everyone pretends to like Buddhism. Then they discover what it entails. People often take Buddhism as more of a relaxed form of Christianity—a Christianity-lite. Unlike the Christian tradition, it doesn't judge you for your crappy decisions regarding your sexual partners and drug-use. It's the go-to, likable religion of today, in the same way that Hinduism did in the '60s when George Harrison jammed on the sitar with Ravi Shankar. In reality, being a Buddhist does not mean you can sit around all day eating pizza, smoking pot, and watching Netflix.

It should be noted that most real Buddhist converts within the U.S. don't have this attitude toward Buddhism. I've had students who'd absolutely reject this understanding of Buddhist practice. That's the thing: they *actually* practice and are coming to have a deep understanding of their spiritual tradition. They recognize and embody the fact that Buddhist practice makes difficult demands on

Thank you! I just made my brother read this. Let me guess, the Buddha doesn't discuss moving back in after college to ruin your younger sister's life either?

THE ACOLYTE

their identity and way of life. After all, Buddhism at its base rejects your belief that we are anything at all. We are nothing, and it's time for us to begin acting like it!

While Buddhism has become a fad in Hollywood, Buddhist practice begins with Siddhartha Gautama, who was a prince somewhere in eastern India. Tradition says that there was a prophecy spoken over him when he was born: either he would be a great religious leader or a great political leader. His father, the king, had no interest in his son becoming a religious leader. So he sequestered Siddhartha to the palace, only letting him know and have contact with the enjoyable things in this life.

Siddhartha, however, grew curious about what lay beyond his castle wall. On three separate occasions, he asked his driver to take him beyond the city walls. While in the world beyond, Siddhartha saw a sick man, an old man, and a dead man for the first time. He came into concrete contact with suffering. Dismayed by these images, Siddhartha set out on his quest to figure out and overcome suffering. He eventually did so, sitting beneath the Bodhi tree in Bodh Gaya some years later, becoming the Buddha, the Enlightened One. His solution to the issue of suffering is customarily offered to us as the Four Noble Truths.

1. Anything can lead to suffering.

You've just bought an ice-cream cone on a beautiful, sunny day. You don't have some crap like mint chocolate-chip, either; you have a godly flavor like peanut-butter-chocolate. You enjoy the cone for ten minutes before the heat outside makes you have to finish. You eat the last bite and find yourself extremely sad. You had such a perfect moment with your ice cream and the sunset, and now it's gone! Heck, you liked the moment so much that you go back for another cone to try to re-create it. Alas, no luck. The ice cream tastes too sweet now and simply gives you a stomach-ache. Life's stupid sometimes.

All can lead to suffering, the Buddha says. If we don't find ourselves directly in the line of suffering by, say, getting bitten by a dog, then we find ourselves experiencing it indirectly by way of a good thing coming to its end, like finishing our ice cream. So our general experience of life culminates in suffering.

2. Attachment is the real cause of suffering.

Look back at your experience with the ice-cream cone. Nothing about eating the cone itself caused suffering. Life with that ice cream is pure, unadulterated bliss. Or at least it could be. The problem comes from the fact that you know that what you're experiencing is bliss, and you don't want it to end, so you attempt to find ways to stave off its coming to an end. You desire this bliss, attach yourself to it, and then attempt to control the world around you in order to stop its movement toward nonbliss.

In other words, you're attached to this sense of bliss. You desire it, and you're willing to act in selfish ways in order to get more of it, like when you cut in line in front of the five-year-old to get your ice cream in the first place. You begin to attempt to control your world in order to gain more of it. You posit yourself as the world's centerpiece. You interpret the world as revolving around you. You try to make yourself a god among mere mortals, demanding that the world fit your needs and desires. You assert yourself.

3. There's an easy solution to the problem of suffering.

I lived in Los Angeles for seven years of my life, and that's six-and-a-half years too long in the megalopolis. I especially abhorred its traffic and had real issues sitting in it during my fifty-five-mile commute between Claremont and Playa Del Rey. From a Buddhist perspective, though, I should have recognized that I was only angry because I thought I deserved more than I did, a road of my own directly to my home, for instance, or at least the right to get home and watch *Game of Thrones* above all the others on the road. The other people on the 405 were just getting in my way for God knows what reason.

Nirvana, or enlightenment, is the solution to this issue. It means freedom from both my hatred of traffic and from my addiction to *Game of*

THE DEACON

If you aren't from LA, know that we put "the" in front of the number for any highway, interstate, freeway, or a road with lots of lanes and a number.

Thrones; more importantly, it means freedom to enjoy my ice cream while I still have it, without worrying about the fact that I'll finish it soon. It really represents freedom from our attachments to our sense of self and the entitlement that comes with it. Enlightenment represents an extinction of the desire to be an entitled self in the passive coming to let go of attachment to all things.

4. The solution's path is pretty difficult.

Easy as the solution is, the implementation is rather difficult. How do you get over yourself and your self-righteous entitlement? If you hate traffic and find yourself very angry in it, reflect on why you're so angry. When you recognize that you're angry because these stupid cars aren't letting you get home to a sweet, sweet episode of *Game of Thrones*, you've understood yourself objectively. Now, catch this insight, observe, and allow your frustration and its causes to sink in. Name them. To whatever degree possible, let them be. And then begin allowing this letting-it-be work into the rest of your life.

I've merely expressed one small part of the idea of meditation found within the Eightfold Path, the Buddha's medicine for this life's sufferings. The Buddha prescribes a lot more that you can do to get yourself over yourself. It remains important to recognize, however, that the goal is to end all desires you might attach yourself to as a self, including any desire to get over desire. Desires will still arise, even if some subside. That's fine. You're going to get hungry; you're going to get jealous; you're going to dislike traffic.

The key is that, if you're extinguishing your sense of self, you'll no longer embrace these desires. They just are and we ought to let them be. After all, if we get angry in traffic, sometimes we can't help it. But if we simply recognize that anger for what it is without giving ourselves to that anger, we won't become consumed by it, embrace it, and feel self-righteously justified in it.

We can push this above insight into its final culmination, which should free us even from Buddhist teachings. An old Zen saying states that if you see the Buddha on the road, kill him. That seems like such a violent saying for the world's most peaceful religious practitioners! Zen thinkers, however, base the saying on a famous parable of similar meaning.

Let's say you're a sojourner stuck on the near shore of a river, which is polluted, filled with three-eyed crocodiles, and tons of mosquitos. You need to get to the other side, where you can see Bambi sticking his head out of a fern, some frolicking, singing rabbits, and trees growing chocolate-covered Gummi-bears. (The Buddha may not have used these exact images.) You need to build a raft to get to the far shore, so you dutifully and meticulously complete it using the sinuous branches to tie broader logs together into a whole. You somehow manage to make a beautiful raft out of some pretty hideous materials.

Avoiding the crocodiles with the dexterity of a catfish, you paddle over to the far shore, at which point the Buddha appears and poses you a question. Picking a Gummibear, he asks whether you need to hang onto the beautiful, life-saving raft or not. You think about how you spent so much time on building it, rowing on it, and that it could be useful again down the road should you come to another dirty river. The Buddha, obviously hovering in a meditative position, wisely suggests that you leave the raft aside—that if you need another down the road, build another! The choice is yours.

THE ELDER

Ever since I saw Keanu Reeves in *Little Buddha* it has significantly impacted all stories of Siddhartha.

Leaving the raft means the same thing as killing the Buddha. It means not getting attached to the instruments that you used to cross that chasm from entitlement to enlightenment. More specifically, both the raft and the Buddha on the road symbolize the Buddha's teachings, the Four Noble Truths, and the tendency to uphold them as something absolute, a doctrine to be obeyed at all costs. The Buddha's teachings are helpful; they're practical; they can show you how to get from nonenlightenment to Nirvana. If you attach yourself to them as truths and try to dogmatically argue for, believe, and teach them, you've lost their function.

In this important regard, if we're to take Buddhist practice seriously, we must recognize that Buddhist practice is not a religion in the sense that it sets up doctrines that you must believe in order to reach Buddhist heaven, which they've strangely named after a '90s grunge band. It unfolds a way of life that will pragmatically help you to see through yourself and become detached from your entitlements, including any religious doctrine, truth, or even the Buddha himself onto which you might be inclined to cling.

Jesus Was Not Actually a Buddhist

I once helped with a fundraiser for the school district in my town. As a purported expert in interreligious dialogue, I led a discussion on the relationship of the Buddha to Christ. Believe me when I say that the table doing whiskey-tastings got a much longer waitlist than mine. As a starting point, I posed a silly question to the group: *Was Jesus actually a Buddhist?* I thought the question was funny and would surely be answered in the negative. I thought we'd open up into a conversation about the important ways that starkly differing religious traditions could learn from one another, but my table resoundingly answered, "Yes, Jesus was a Buddhist!" For the sake of decorum, I accepted my defeat that night and proceeded with the long night and the conversation that emerged.

This point is extremely important when we talk interreligious dialogue. Buddhism often gets framed as Christianity-lite. Or, as it did at my table that night, Christianity is considered a form of Western Buddhism.

Neither position is correct. Instead, we should take up the postmodern affirmation of difference, acknowledging that we really believe importantly different things.

After all, the Christian faith is interested in the pursuit of truth; Buddhist practice pursues pragmatic teachings, enjoining us to ignore the notion of truth since it can get in our way of enlightenment. The Christian faith believes that truth culminates in God, the creator of all things; Buddhist practice may agree, and says that for the same reason, you should probably ignore God because any thought about God, or truth, will hinder your enlightenment. The Christian faith believes that heaven means existence in the full light of God's being; Buddhist practice accepts the death of all things and attempts to make its followers' deaths permanent. The Christian faith says suffering in the world was never supposed to be and that God has come to us to fix what's at issue; Buddhist practice says that we merely need to learn to contend with suffering properly by getting over ourselves. Christian salvation reforms who we are so that we might live properly in the in-breaking kingdom of God; Buddhist enlightenment gives itself over to nothingness so that, whatever may happen, "you" will no longer be perturbed. Jesus called God "Abba," passionately trying to bring his good and peace-seeking will unto the earth; the Buddha, for fear of igniting desire and more suffering, sat silent in front of the young seeker who asked the Buddha whether or not there was a God.

We are dealing with two very different religions, and I can see no way to unite them into the coexist option, at least not without doing horrible violence to both religions. After all, it seems to me that the worst thing I could tell a

Buddhist nun is that, in her meditations, she's really secretly leading the Israelites with Moses out of Egypt and into the Promised Land. No, we have to take people at their word that they're up to something different than us. This fact doesn't mean that we can't be in fruitful dialogue with one another. In fact, recognizing the real differences between these standpoints may illuminate something important.

Is the real problem the desire to coexist? What you are highlighting seems to really be the

THE DEACON

desire to erase the difference between religions rather than preserving the differences in peace.

Since we're talking bumper stickers, let me bring up another that can begin giving us an alternative route to the coexist sticker when it comes to interreligious dialogue. I'm talking, of course, about "These Colors Don't Run!" I've often chuckled at the particular form of patriotism the sticker elicits. It implies that the U.S. should refuse to back down from a fight—*any* fight—regardless of its justice or necessity. But let's flip that script and apply it positively to interreligious dialogue.

First, there's no need to run from dialogue with those who disagree with us. In fact, dialogue-in-difference poses no threat whatsoever and can even be very helpful. Second, I'm proposing that dialogue need not wistfully blend traditions into a form of cafeteria religion as coexisters want to do. I'm asking that persons interested in true dialogue allow themselves to be informed by a religious position that is *completely different* from their own tradition, but also potentially very helpful to them.

THE ELDER

If you grew up in the South and weren't evangelical you would probably prefer a neighbor with a coexist sticker than one about a flag not running.

For example, I have picked up some very important insights from Buddhist thought, and they don't even have to do with the ability to hold a downward dog longer or to hit an extra chin-up. Rather, I learned how entitled I am. Not that I would be considered particularly entitled by our social understandings. I'm not a control freak; I'm fairly generous; and I try not to complain too much. I'm actually relaxed about most things other than traveling and traveling in traffic, both of which turn me into a two-year-old who needs a snack. Entitlement, though, seems to reside eternally within my—really, everyone's—heart. We all want the world; we want to own it and make it ours for taking. We want to think of ourselves, our work, our goals as more important than they are. But they're really not that important, at least not as much as we aggrandize them to be. We ourselves—our goals and desires—are not all that important.

This Buddhist insight has not turned me into a Buddhist, even if I have a great appreciation for the tradition. It has reopened me to that important gospel teaching: "not my will but yours." We make that prayer halfheartedly, and we generally mean it in the context of God as a vending-machine God: "God, please let it be your will that I can sport a sweet 'stache while driving a '72 Camaro." If we reinterpret the prayer from the standpoint of detachment, we open the prayer to its truth as well: that we need simply to let things be. We must not try to control the world and force it to fit our desires. We must, instead, offer our wills back to God and allow these wills to be reformed by way of Joan of Arc and her interruption of our expectations.

Near- or Far-Sighted?

We've established a potential way in which we might relate to differing religions and do so with honesty, but I think we're still faced with a big, fat "Who cares?" We need to return to the original set of questions: How do we believe what we do in light of varying religious beliefs and modes of God-talk around the world, how do we conceptualize and talk to others of these differing traditions, and what justifies our sticking to our own religious traditions after these talks? We just partially answered the second question regarding how we might talk to persons of other traditions: honestly and without simply giving away our tradition. But in answering it, I did so with an implied answer to the first and third questions in mind.

The first question asked how we can justifiably believe the things we believe in light of varying religious beliefs and modes of God-talk around the world. I begin answering it by noting that we have the religious beliefs that we do because we've been steeped in the bourbon barrel of tradition, and our minds are always at least partially, if not fully, bound to the traditions from whence we've come. We oftentimes use that as a negative statement, claiming that the lenses that tradition puts on us blind us to the world outside that tradition. While we can find truth in the sentiment, it goes wrong in two ways.

Few persons who wear glasses complain about the better sight glasses bring. Glasses may be annoying at points, and they may even begin to distort your vision when the prescription is off. But a good pair of glasses helps those who are either near- or far-sighted to see the world around them, and that's a good thing. Tradition works similarly.

THE DEACON

Which tradition is the stylish equivalent to thick black hipster framed glasses?

Tradition, especially religious tradition, forms a lens for us, a way of seeing the world. We're then very often tempted to talk about how it biases us, and about how we need to overcome this tradition. But we do so while ignoring the fact that this very tradition has a penchant for self-critique, which derives from both the Hebrew prophetic and Socratic traditions.

I'm saying that tradition doesn't necessarily obscure the truth. Instead, tradition functions as the very lens that opens our eyes to the truth in the first place. The lense of tradition acts as the lenses of glasses, clarifying the world in which we live and giving us access to its meaning and truth. We believe what we do because these traditions have opened us to the truth in the first place. But such a belief can't be the lip-service belief brought by the coexister; it must be a fully-fledged belief that the very lenses of tradition themselves participate in the truth, drawing us into it. It's a belief, in fact, that these lenses do so very helpfully and well, maybe even better than anyone else's lenses.

As I've been arguing, there's no way to avoid tradition. It defines us, even when we don't want it to. This is why the Dalai Lama says, "I always tell my Western friends that it is best to keep your own tradition. Changing religion is not easy and sometimes causes confusion. You must value your tradition and honor your own religion."[2] Because of this fact, when we try to deny that we're engaging in something like interreligious dialogue out of our own tradition, we only reaffirm the fact that we're caught in tradition in the first place precisely because we speak this concern out of a concern for our tradition!

This idea points to the fact that, at least as a Christian, I engage in interreligious dialogue not as a way around tradition but because, through tradition and its truth, I feel called by a God who acts out of love, calling me to the same in the process. I really believe that idea, and I don't set it on the backburner by submitting it to other interpretations when taking the religious other seriously; I embrace it all the more. I take up that love—a movement beyond myself in such a way that I can take another seriously as who they are rather than who I want them to be. I apply that love to my situation—I'm faced with a religious other who deserves to be understood where she stands. I live out that love—I accept that many of my desires in this world are bound up with a sinful sense of selfishness, which I relearned through my Buddhist friends.

THE BISHOP

Yes! I think I have felt this without knowing how to say it. It's just my diaconate meetings are interreligious.

What I'm getting at pushes us now in the direction of answering our third concern. I've been implying that the most difficult problem facing us in a religiously pluralistic world pertains to the question of how we can justifiably prioritize our own religious beliefs above others. I'm questioning ultimately why I should take any God-talk that *I* might engage in throughout this book seriously, knowing that there are so many who speak differently and seem to have as much of a say on God as I do. But I believe that I'm absolutely justified in holding to the priority because any denial of it already depends on the tradition that defines me. After all, I can affirm or reject my tradition only as based in my tradition, only in knowing it so well that I can see what's actually, and not what I'm told by my professors is, wrong with it.

If I deny my reliance on my tradition, I end up cutting myself off from any real dialogue with others and

> This is one of the reasons I get frustrated with popular atheist criticisms of God. I rarely have encountered the God they are denying and usually feel they have trivialized my own tradition. Of course apologists do the same to them.

THE DEACON

the possibility of really learning something from them. I cut myself off from the source of taking others seriously in their own terms. I end up cutting off love. Ultimately, if I deny the realities of my own tradition, I bind myself to a paradox: because I know nothing about the tradition that already influences me, I become a slave to it. I become so closely defined by my tradition that I'm incapable of understanding where my tradition influences me, focuses my attention, and defines my perceptions. I thereby close myself off from any real transcendence from it, denying myself the beauty of interreligious dialogue, which ought to bring to us an ability to think through ourselves from an outside perspective. Strangely, the ability for me to take the religious other seriously as they are and not how I want them to be depends on me prioritizing my tradition and the love bound up with it.

So let's take our God-talk seriously, learn what we can from Buddhists, and then leave them alone. Let's stop trying to make them into something that they're not:

Christians-lite. Let's, rather, empathetically embrace them in their real difference, knowing there's much there to learn and much there to reject.

7

Becoming a More Consistent Atheist

We've talked a lot about God and concepts of God, but we've not once brought up whether we actually have anything to talk about! For all we know, we may be engaging in a potentially interesting but utterly pointless conversation akin to whether minotaurs prefer ice cream or hummus. Perhaps we've put the cart before the unicorn, but we can certainly take the question up now by trying to decipher whether or not God exists, on what grounds God may exist, and on what grounds God may not exist.

This lattermost question is especially important. Today's reasons for rejecting an intellectual search for God often take the form of an absurd but culturally acceptable idea I call *science worship* (or *naturalism* in philosophical and beach-going circles alike). Science worshipers bow at the idol of measurement. They pour out libations to science from the beaker and the test-tube and then offer science sweet incense on petri dishes. They sacrifice at the altar of empirical data. That is, science-worshipers tend to believe truth only ever emerges within a so-called scientific context. The problem is that science worshipers follow a false god, even if there's none to follow.

THE DEACON

So do frat boys.
Never mind.

Let's take a look at where reasonable belief in God potentially goes right, and where we culturally misdiagnose the issues at stake through science-worship. In the process, I'll offer a serious suggestion to help science-worshiping-style atheists to find a more appropriate ground upon which to ground a *real* atheism, one that I'll take up more fully in the next chapter. This real atheism represents an atheism that, I'll confess, has certainly tempted me and will continue to do so. After all, when real issues are raised, then real questions are at stake. That becomes true of atheism once we move past science worship.

Miyagi-God's Existence

When I was about six, I figured out the Santa hoax. As I thought through all the bits and pieces that my parents, the media, and my kindergarten peers told me, nothing added up. After all, Christmas was Jesus's birthday, and

Jesus awesomely decided to give *us* his presence/presents for his birthday. So I was told. Santa could've been delivering these presents on Jesus's behalf, but, frankly, never once had I seen a Greek saint on the same sleigh, or even in the same picture, as a Norwegian Hippie!

I settled my query. Obviously there's a Jesus. Obviously, then, there can be no Santa. Therefore, six-year-olds are hilarious.

Atheists tend to treat belief in God like we treat belief in Santa: fine for a child but not for any reasonable adult. If we don't take that atheist position, then we take the only alternative that we know, the position of faith. By *faith*, we usually mean blind-willed belief. In this context, faith somehow has more power than does reason; and God, as a cosmic vending machine, will reward us for believing despite the fact that, rationally, we shouldn't believe. The problem is that this whole setup is wrong, even if it tends to be the only setup that we know.

In a fundamental and very basic way, it's not that difficult to recognize the existence of God, at least of a particular kind and under certain constraints. I'm not talking about the understandings of God that many believers and atheists share: say, the muscled Old-Man River, which is a lot more difficult to affirm. However, the beginnings of Miyagi-God—that is, God as the highest reality or God as identity itself—far from being irrational, cannot be reasonably avoided. We've simply socialized ourselves into thinking this belief is fundamentally difficult, or else we've never taken our respect for reason to its ultimate end. Probably both.

To claim that God exists at the level I'm claiming does not presume that we're talking about the Christian God,

THE ACOLYTE

I think I am a bit too postmodern to hear you through your confidence. Let me read some Foucault real quick and I'll be back.

Jewish God, or Muslim God, nor is this the God of the average, everyday churchgoer, whose concept of God can be summed up in a sense of folk-religiosity that we've come to call shredded Old-Man River God. In fact, in my philosophy of God and religion course, several of my theology students have told me that in order to begin getting their minds around this idea of God, they need to separate out their spirituality from these philosophical ways of talking, which attests to how different this God is in terms of the usual ways we want to talk about God. After all,

THE BISHOP

I can imagine that kind of advice not working well during adult education hour at church.

we're talking about the God of reason, the God of the philosophers. This God grounds all truth, identity, goodness, and beauty. This God is Miyagi. On these grounds, I absolutely affirm this separation of spirituality and thought in my students on one condition: that they're willing to revisit and revise what they think it means to be spiritual in light of the truths that emerge here philosophically.

Miyagi-God is absolute identity and the highest reality. Miyagi-God is an absolute stability, and under a certain condition, we have to admit that this God exists as the world's stability. That condition emerges if we can find in our lives what's called an *unqualified truth*. Don't let the name throw you off. An unqualified truth is a truth that we *must* affirm under any and all circumstances, cultural or otherwise. We don't get to add qualifiers to the statement such as "Christmas *to me* means eating cookies" or "*in this context*, you make me sick." Unqualified truths have no qualifiers attached.

I am guessing you scratch the word "like" out of a bunch of Miyagi-God term papers.

THE ACOLYTE

A lot of philosophers talk about math as producing unqualified truths. 2 and 2 equals 4 no matter what your culture, or what planet you're on. That's why many of the efforts to communicate with extraterrestrials in the '70s often included mathematical equations and music, the latter of which is just math expressed through vibration. Anyone can potentially understand math because it transcends culture, space, and time. For God, however, we can do better than a math equation in terms of asserting an unqualified truth.

For instance, we already always affirm the existence and meaningfulness of the concept of truth. I say that because, even in directly denying truth, we're actually claiming a truth *for ourselves*. We're claiming to have found the truth that truth has no existence or meaning. In our denial of the existence of truth, we actually affirm another truth! Frankly, that point is unqualified in the same way that 2 and 2 make 4: under any circumstance, we must admit that there is something like truth.

That point may seem unconvincing at first, but try leveling some arguments against my portrayal of the truth of truth. Here are a few common ones. I can take a sociological stance and argue that I've simply been socialized into thinking that such a truth exists. I respond that the accuser must then believe himself to be socialized into thinking he's correct, unless he's willing to give his position an air of truth. Such a willingness would merely bring the critic back to my original claim: that we affirm that truth as such exists in an unqualified manner, even if we have nothing other than this one truth.

Or take the semantic rejection. A critic can claim that I'm merely stringing a series of words together, but it would be foolish to think that words have anything to do with reality. Words are just words, ways of expressing ourselves, and perhaps our preferences, but never truths. No doubt, my new accuser does the same as the last: she thinks that she knows something real about language in her language, but then denies that anyone else can know anything true through language. I hope you see the issue.

Or finally, some science-worshiping philosophers take something like a biological-evolutionary argument. Words, ideas, concepts, and beliefs all evolve for the sake of our survival but not with a sense of truth in mind. We may believe we have the truth, but we don't: we have instinct, they would argue. No doubt, however, this science-worshiping critic doesn't believe that his words about evolution are merely a matter of survival but convey something true. This critic can't have his cake and eat it too: either our words and beliefs gain us truth, or they gain us some useful ideas helpful for surviving but gaining us truth, at best, by accident. This critic comes to the truths of the evolutionary rationale because they're useful for survival, but the critic can never know them to be true, only helpful.

If you weren't Catholic I would be expecting a John 14:6 reference next. #IAMtheWAY

THE DEACON

I could produce a number of other examples on this list, but the crux of the claim that the truth of truth is unqualified rests on a particular understanding of truth, which means the correspondence or correctness between the way we conceive of something and the way that something works out in reality. Truth is a correspondence between thought and being. To the degree that we talk and intend to discuss anything of substance, we're always at least partially talking about reality, even when we talk about our words, which are themselves very real. We cannot get out of this affirmation without affirming something else we think is correct in its place.

What I want to convey is that from this complicated set of thoughts, we can affirm Miyagi-God. After all, we defined Miyagi as the absolute stability point undergirding all things, the pulsating identity that allows all things to be. If truth is the correspondence between our concepts and reality, and if we can produce an unqualified truth, Miyagi, as this stability point, is necessary to affirm this absolutely stable and unqualified truth. An unqualified truth depends on an unqualified reality or Miyagi.

I consider myself a fallibilist, which is quite the awesome term, I know! What this means is that I'm willing to admit when I'm wrong. I don't cling dogmatically to an idea because I need the idea. I'm willing to revise ideas in light of better ones, knowing the limitations of my own thinking. In this way, I don't *need* to show that God exists for any personal reason. I don't think this knowledge will "save" anyone, and I won't get credit for it in heaven. In some ways, showing this only makes my life harder as a theologian, which is especially true in the context of what we'll call the problem of evil and the question of whether we should care about this God. I simply think it's true that we can affirm in a very limited way God's existence, and I've come to assent to this belief on a very peculiar ground: I'm fallibilistic about my fallibilism. Even though I'm inclined to believe in the limitations of knowledge, I've also come to accept on fallibilistic grounds that there are some ideas that absolutely depend on the existence of Miyagi. In this way, I refuse to engage a falsely humble

I think there should be a spiritual discipline called cultivating conscious fallibilism. It would significantly detoxify my facebook feed.

THE ELDER

and pretentious disavowal of the possibility of this kind of knowledge, which persons oftentimes use to attempt to move beyond this form of argumentation.

Some of the other reasons for ignoring this type of argument are less honest and more annoying. People often like to ask three silly questions that they believe make them sound skeptically intelligent when arguing against the possibility of reasonably arguing for God's existence: (1) If there's a God who creates everything, who creates God?; (2) If God can do anything, can God create a mountain that he can't lift?; and (3) How about you give me some real, empirical proof for this crappy argument? In response to these questions, I simply say that (1) no one creates God because God is the very act of absolute identity on which any other identity depends and thus must be uncreated; (2) no, God cannot create a mountain that he can't lift, and that question would only make sense if I were arguing for Jersey Shore, whose omnipotence means "can do anything"; and (3) it's time to get over empiricism.

It's this third question that's the most powerful in contemporary persons' minds, and throughout the rest of the chapter I'd like to show you why this question simply fails to be important.

On Arguing with "That Guy"

I absolutely love Socrates. The man's hilariously bombastic and an expression of true intellectual humility, both at once. The *Gorgias* represents a favorite dialogue of mine and, in it, Socrates is heartily at work arguing with the nihilist, Callicles, among other pernicious conversation partners. He's convincing Callicles that the tyrant of a city stands in a worse spot than a good person whom the tyrant actively tortures, which seems really counterintuitive, and Callicles constantly attempts to argue the opposite. Exasperated by Socrates' arguments, Callicles laments, "I don't know how it is that I think you're right, Socrates, but the thing that happens to most people has happened to me: I'm not really convinced by you." Callicles thinks Socrates is "that guy."[1]

That guy represents a person you know well. He's the guy who won't shut up in class or in a meeting, who simply loves to hear himself talk. He's that guy who argues with you nonstop, that guy who seems so smugly self-confident that you'll do anything not to agree with him. We've all been in Callicles' place, even if we lack his awesome name. We know his experience well.

Most of us have found ourselves in an argument where we *should* agree with our conversation partner, and we even acquiesce in our private thoughts to that guy's arguments, or at least we come to admit that there's something to that guy's thoughts. Out of pride and a defiant will, however, we stand with Callicles and say to ourselves, "I maybe intellectually agree with that guy, but I refuse to be convinced, mainly because he's an ass."

Maybe anyone trying to argue for the existence of God and doing so with a modicum of plausibility stands

I was recently reading a book about God and thought something similar.

THE BISHOP

in the position of being that guy today. Maybe I'm being that guy. After all, you can no doubt reach a point of saying to yourself, "I understand what this idiot is saying, and there's unfortunately something to it, but there's absolutely no way I'm acquiescing to his point. I have my own beliefs and opinions, man!"

The truth may be that this guy—like Socrates—actually has a reasonable and convincing point to make, and we'd be intelligent to listen despite our pride. Like Callicles, we're often unwilling to see what that reality is because the reality we face contradicts some assumption that we've bit into hook, line, and sinker. This assumption that we use to reject any willingness to listen stems from that so-called intelligent question, "Can you give me some real, empirical proof for this crappy argument?" You see, we assume that we should only take seriously the existence of things that are palpable or measurable; we tend to think that only science has meaningful answers to our perplexing troubles and questions.

This belief is very wrong.

Jenga and Science-Worship

When I was in high school, we didn't yet have smart phones, so we didn't sit around next to each other playing on the stupid things. We did have awesome laser-tag sets, movies, videogames, and board games. On Friday and Saturday nights, my friends and I would happily engage in a few, if not all four, of our time-honored, weekend activities. Obviously, I really wasn't a part of a wild crew in high school.

When it rained, which in Seattle is often, Jenga became our board game of choice, which probably stemmed from its interactive nature. This interaction was important because in the few times we managed to get some lady-friends to hang out with us, I'd find ways to awkwardly flirt with them through the game's conversation-forcing mayhem. One flirting method I used was obvious: I'd cause my love-interest to lose at Jenga by setting her up through my honed Jenga skills with a carefully extracted block. She'd try to remove the next one, and wham!, the tower came down. In the collapse of the tower, I thought that the young woman would fall immediately in love with me. Should that strategy fail, however, I'd pull a reversal. This time, I'd make the Jenga tower to fall on purpose so that I could look like the goofy nice-guy—you know, the stereotype that gets *all* the girls.

I'm not saying I was good at flirting, or, frankly, that I've ever gotten any better. (Luckily, I still managed to get married.) I have, however, retained my propensity for and skill at Jenga, and I want to play Jenga with this science-worshiping position by extracting some of the important blocks that present themselves in today's culture.

The first Jenga-block that I'd like to extract represents a cartoonish but important one that a few folks still believe. It'll setup future analyses and block-extractions. Variations of this position have been held to by persons

THE ACOLYTE

I have to say I would rather play Jenga on a date than *Dance Dance Revolution*. It is hard to take anyone playing that game seriously.

such as David Hume, Auguste Comte, Bertrand Russell, A. J. Ayer, and Daniel Dennett. The block is composed of a science-worship in the extreme, one that draws understandable but contradictory conclusions.

This brand of science-worshiping calls any idea that is empirically verifiable and repeatable a *fact* and anything beyond the empirically measurable "nonsense." It holds that ideas we can operate on in a laboratory have some oomph to them, and our belief in them is reasonable. Ideas that we cannot operate on in a laboratory are opinions at best and superstitious at worst. They lack oomph. Such is God for the science-worshiper.

God is simply a hypothesis that we don't need any longer. We used to believe in the importance of God prior to the advent of science because God could fill in the explanatory gaps of our knowledge. Don't know what causes lightning? Attribute it to God and take some darn cover! Don't know when a volcano will blow? Of course you don't! God's unpredictable, and the magma getting near your foot is obviously a consequence of God's wrath. However, with the emergence of the explanatory sciences, science-worshipers believe that we can throw out this byproduct of our civilization, namely, the God hypothesis. To be honest, we actually can in terms of persons who try to explain direct phenomenon in terms of God's direct interventions with nature, but the reason the science-worshiper throws God out pertains to his indecipherable and unmeasurable qualities. From this position, God comes to represent an idea clung to by weak-willed people who won't give up their childhood ideas for scientific adulthood.

Let's get to some Jenga.

The first block to be removed is the foundation of the science-worshiper's notion of truth: items that are observable, measurable, or somehow empirically verifiable. If something's worth talking about at the level of truth, we'd better be able to submit that thing either to direct observation or to an empirical experiment to see what it really is. The simple problem with this definition of truth is one that came to be recognized by even its starkest proponents in the twentieth-century positivist circles: this very criterion for truth isn't itself observable, measurable, or empirically verifiable; it does not and cannot abide by its own criterion for truth. Science-worshipers simply assert it based either on a set of cultural assumptions into which they've been indoctrinated, or based on something like the practical success of the sciences in altering and transforming our world.

Neither motivation, however, fulfills its own criteria of what makes for a fact, a truth statement, or a reasonable position. Neither motivation actually gives us an observable, measurable, or empirically verified experiment that shows definitively, given the available data, that this statement is the best possible statement concerning truth. It

Luckily God inspired high-quality cinema like *God Is Not Dead* to witness to these Science-Worshiping Atheists! (I am being sarcastic. That movie might be a secret New Atheist recruiting tool.)

THE DEACON

simply gives us an assumption, which somehow still holds great sway in certain science-worshiping circles in the face of thousands of years' worth of philosophical refutation of these kinds of theories and ideas.[2]

Read the footnote. Then imagine the fun conversations you could have with a *Bringing Sextus Back* shirt.

THE ACOLYTE

The Second Jenga-Block: A Tepid Science-Worship

Some brilliant men and women in the history of philosophy have embraced the above position, and I can't blame them. They saw the sciences transforming the world, giving us new medicines like penicillin and antibiotics that allowed us to survive the simple cuts that threatened us with sepsis before; they saw the sciences creating power-plants and harnessing the energy of nature so that people could heat their homes without spending all their waking hours cutting wood; they saw flight—human-freaking-flight and space-adventures! And they also saw a dog-matic church saying that if you put up a lightning rod, you're sinfully taking away the ability of God (that is, Jersey Shore-God) to punish you for your other sins. I'm not kidding on that last bit. Certain Philadelphia-area preachers actually said that about ol' Ben Franklin's lightning-attracting invention.

I can't blame these early science-worshiping men and women for their stance. They were trying to take away the tool of churchgoing dictators to instill fear in the general populace about certain technological advances that the dictators thought ran counter to theological teaching. They were trying to find freedom to live better, longer, and more hospitable lives. The only alternative to the science-worship they advocated seemed to be a grumpy dogmatism.

Still, the position is wrong, and while people don't tend to directly hold this position explicitly anymore, it has had cultural sway in the West, remaining subtly influential in the same way that Zeus gives us our conception of God as a shredded Old-Man River. Here's how: Think of the first explanation that tends to come to someone's mind when they're asked about what makes a person smart or not. A lot of the thoughts that emerge pertain to genetics. We look to genes for everything today, including how much you're able to love your dog's breath to how much weight you'll put on by eating berries. We reduce love to the idea of a gene and its pre-made, material possibilities all the time. For example, for a small price you can compare body odor genes to determine whether you're compatible to marry someone. Lord knows that genes trump conversation, especially when looking for love! The implication is that love is merely genetic fan-fiction useful for getting us to sow our oats and continue our genetic lineage, and we're at least inclined to buy it.

Maybe a practitioner of scientism could use this as a pick-up line, "How would you like to make  **THE DEACON** romantic genetic fan-fiction with me? I got a meme you just have to explore."

Another scenario: next time you're in the airport, grab a *Men's Health* magazine. In it, you'll find some awesome nutritional tips. For instance, we're told to "think lean" because it's "mind over fatter: considering yourself pudgy could increase both your poundage and BMI, a British study suggests."[3] Thank the God of science that a "study," which connotes a scientific study, has suggested this fact, especially one completed with a cool, authority-producing accent like the Brits have! Or take a look at "The MetaShred program is more than just a nine-DVD workout plan; it's a revolutionary fitness system *scientifically designed* to make every minute of your training session more effective."[4] So long as it's "scientifically designed," which I haven't a clue how to interpret, we're good with it.

Science-worship today is not so much explicitly worship anymore. Few are trying to set up a church of science. Rather, the language of the sciences has come to embed itself so deeply in our minds that we fall under two chemically induced spells. The first is that we tend to believe statements bolstered by "clinical study" or "scientifically proven" are true. I'm not claiming that we willingly believe these things, but I'm suggesting that we flip past them in such a way that we simply give them a nod and a shake, saying "hmm, that's interesting," with no questions asked.

This brings up the second point: we skip past these statements in such a way that we wouldn't do when a doofus like me claims he can prettily easily show the necessity of Miyagi-God, but we'd immediately consider the idea, so long as it was said by a scientist, or at least someone who can talk pseudo-physics. We're culturally uncomfortable with philosophical types of claims I'm making, and we're immediately skeptical of them in a manner proportionate to how quickly we accept "scientific studies" as giving us facts.

In fact, we feel like Callicles did with Socrates: even if we can intellectually assent to the idea, we just can't bring ourselves to really admit to it. That's not a conscious choice; that's the cultural aftermath of the science-worshiping figures who came before us and swayed culture away from metaphysics and toward medicine. The aftermath of science-worship is having a difficult time caring about any talk of the real existence of God one way or another, which extends itself into a sort of practical atheism that says "meh" to any such claims about God's truthful being.

Let's remove this second Jenga-block. We'll do it very simply: by affirming the importance of critical thought in all things, which means questioning so-called philosophical conclusions and so-called scientific studies alike. For instance, there are a number of questions with the above demonstration of God's existence, and they should be pressed. Does my having to admit to truth mean I have to admit to an unqualified truth? Do aliens from other planets actually experience this unqualified truth? Does truth actually mean correspondence? To be honest, asking critical questions in this way comes easy to us, and we naturally find ourselves questioning philosophical positions in just such a way. We now need to ask questions of the sciences and those who make divine use of the sciences' names.

After all, pop-nutritional science relies explicitly on correlation and not causation to make claims. Persons who drink a glass of red wine a night may live longer, but it may be because persons who drink a glass of red wine at night (1) don't drink any more than that and (2) eat nothing but kale salads. I mean only to say that in the same way a religious leader used to be able to say, "God says . . ." and have everyone fall in line, now we only need to say, "this study shows . . ." for the same effect, and neither position should sway us.

This point brings me to my third and final Jenga-block: that we tend to misunderstand the sciences and what they do.

The Third Jenga-Block: Truth in the Sciences

During the fall of 2015 in a course called *Violence and Atonement*, I tried to explain to my students what bad Christian

THE BISHOP

Ten out of ten bishops agree that a glass of red wine and kale salad are the perfect accompaniment to finishing your sermon on Saturday evening.

apologetics consists of. I directed them to a YouTube video starring Kirk Cameron and Ray Comfort about the wonderful, God-given design of bananas. I honestly have no clue whether this video's serious, but Comfort argues that the banana displays an unmistakable design that disallows us to believe in anything other than a provident, nature-ordering God. The video is also uncomfortably phallic, which I completely forgot about when I started showing it. Upon some inadvertent sexual references by this dynamic duo, I raced to the front of the room, red-faced, to turn the video off. My class laughed hysterically. It turns out I didn't merely display a piece of bad Christian apologetics; I found a semi-pornographic example.

My students have not let me live this moment down since.

THE ACOLYTE

I just googled that. It has altered my day.

Some forms of Christian apologetics have taken up the scientific sword, which is a lot like Paul's shield of righteousness only with more Bunsen burners attached. They want to ward away the folks hell-bent on science-worshiping God away. They do so by trying to show that only a designer could have created the proportions between things like gravity and anvils such that anvils drop perfectly on Wiley Coyote's head, or they argue that God creates bananas that are perfectly designed to fit into a backpack for later consumption. In doing so, however, these Christian apologists have given themselves over to the same unflappable mistake that the science-worshipers also buy into: that science can say anything, pro or con, about God. Allow me a digression on the nature of reason and our relationship to it because, through it, I'd like to set this science-story straight.

In December of 2013, soon after my wife had become pregnant, we decided to make a road trip together to Yellowstone to see the veritable zoo of animals that make their way into the Lamar Valley during the winter months. After a day of wolf- and moose-watching, we grabbed a hotel room in Bozeman, calling it a night. Or so I thought. I was awoken around 2 a.m. by a phone call from our house-alarm company. You see, when I found out we were having a baby, I went into a hyper-protective mode for a little bit and insisted to my wife that we install an alarm in case someone broke into our home when I was traveling. She responded that we live in the middle of Montana, where crime-rate is in the negatives. People here break into other people's homes and put their own jewelry in the safes! Unfortunately, I won that argument only out of the sheer vehemence of my insecurity at the time, and because of my need to feel like a protector of the home. We got the alarm service.

One of the motion sensors had gone off, and this worried me. Motion sensors function as a second resort to door sensors, setting the alarm off if any animal over thirty pounds walks by them. We have a couple of cats, one of which is a hefty but muscular 16.6 pounds, so our Boomer shouldn't have set the alarm off, but I had to make a quick choice with the alarm company: have them call the police to do a check or hypothesize that it was the cat. I went with the cat, got off the phone, and lay there awake all night, wondering if I'd made the right judgment. There was only one way to find out.

When we got home the next day, I went into our house first and looked around. The cats were fine, no windows were broken, and no doors had been pried ajar. Neither did I notice any bearded men lying on our couch watching TV or showering, or even a fat, forty-pound raccoon running through our place wreaking havoc. According to the data in front of me, no person had broken into our home. Everything was just the same as we left it. I *did* go and read up on the motion sensors, and noted that they're supposed to be placed at least four to six feet above the ground, far away from all shelves where something like a cat couldn't jump up and get right in front of them to set off the alarm. My sensor was sitting on a bookshelf that my cats liked to climb.

It turns out I had made the right call to leave the police alone. More importantly, I also came to a true-enough insight in the investigation: the cats had likely set the alarm off. You see, truth simply stands for a model that best accounts for the data at hand. Some models can account for the data in an unqualified and absolute manner, which we call unqualified truths; others can only account for the data with a sense of probability, which we call reasoned opinions. Both the type of commonsense insight I came to about my cats and scientific modeling are of the reasoned-opinion types of truth. That we have and pursue truth and cannot avoid doing so is of the unqualified and absolute variety.

Is it wrong that I am judging you for having a cat? I tend to trust people with dogs.

THE DEACON

I've said already that truth means the correspondence between our concepts and the reality they convey. The process by means of which we come to truth, while difficult enough to actually perform, is simple enough to explain. We come up with a hypothesis or a model to account for the data in front of us such as, "my cats set off my alarm." We ask a bunch of questions that would attempt to poke a hole in that model: "Did I come home to a hobo sleeping on my couch, or a coyote bathing in my bathroom?" If answers to these questions are yes, then we've poked a hole. The hobo or the coyote set off the alarm. If they don't poke a hole, but we know that there are other possible questions we haven't asked, we've gotten an insight that's true-enough, which is called a reasoned opinion. If we find ourselves in a spot where ideas we deny depend on the very ideas they affirm, such as the idea of truth I've been discussing, then we have an unqualified truth. Any which way we look at it, truth merely represents a model that we've tested in enough ways that we say about it, sure!

I bring all these points up about the truth for a very simple reason: scientific truth operates by way of these same processes as the practical insight above but with very specific concerns in mind. Scientific truths aren't after commonsense truths or metaphysical truths, although they come to their conclusions in the same basic way; they're interested in truths that account for a very specific kind of data, namely, data that pertain *only* to material things and can be measured and verified through reproduction. In other words, the sciences reduce their search for the truth to measurable phenomena in the material world: they look for material constancy in things. These insights, in turn, yield for us ways to manipulate those things to better serve us, such as by finding new microorganisms that have evolved natural defenses against bacteria, which we can cultivate into new antibiotics. We get technology.

Finally, this: the sciences yield for us reasoned opinions, to be sure, but they give us these with very specific criteria in mind: material reproducibility and constancy. Anything outside of these criteria, the sciences don't have anything positive or negative to say about one way or another. They are and should be silent about such things, including the possibility or impossibility of God, who's neither material, measurable, nor reproducible.[5]

That said, I think that this block forms the final one for science-worship. It simply recognizes the sciences for what they are: an amazing and effective way of looking at the material world, which ultimately yields us the technologies to live longer and more comfortably. They don't say a damned bit else—not about God, not about us, and not about the meaning of dogs—and they don't need to in order to be valuable nonetheless. Any affirmation or rejection of the possibility of God from the standpoint of the sciences simply misses the point of the sciences altogether.

Tupac vs. Macklemore

An intellectual assent to acknowledging the existence of Miyagi-God doesn't give us a reason to walk away from the sciences. That would be an absurd conclusion. After all, I'm having solar panels installed on my roof, and these wonderful and renewable energy harvesters stem from the minds of ingenious scientists who find ways to use things like silicon to harness the power of the sun. In turn, this allows me to gather electricity to put on a mesmerizing episode of *Sesame Street* and eke out just one, five-minute shower without my two-year-old daughter destroying a book, flashlight, or anything else she can get her hands on when I'm not looking.

Neither do I want to neglect the fact that the sciences are currently bastions of many creative individuals coming up with ingenious ways to think through chemical and biological processes, not for any technological end but for the same reason I like to think: as something worth doing for its own sake. No, we don't get to run away from science because of Miyagi; we simply have to rethink what the sciences are, what they mean, and how seriously we should take some of their worshipers' broader claims.

Still, I'd be remiss to say that, because science-worship has no grounds, atheistic ideas go away. That's far from the case. The critique must be reenvisioned more helpfully. To this end, I'd like to point out that I've come to appreciate a lot of rap albums decorated with the infamous parental advisory warning, at least ones from the '90s and 2000s. I enjoy listening to Tupac and Outkast; I like the Roots and the Wu Tang Clan. I even like Eminem, although he's a bit too new for me.

I feel like a *total poser* since my listening habits generally stray toward New Orleans jazz (a favorite of all aging, white intellectuals), the Zac Brown Band, and just a little bit of Pentatonix around Christmas time. I don't doubt that these rap artists would kindly but firmly ask me to listen to someone else. Still, I've come to see something that I never could grasp as a younger man: that these artists tell authentic stories about their own experiences as the social pariahs of a broader culture—as persons dejected and confined to the ghettos of L.A., Atlanta, or Detroit.

I also think they have some sick beats.

I contrast these artists with Macklemore. I've got nothing against Macklemore—I enjoyed the song about him having a wolf on his noggin, and he has nothing close to a bad message in his songs. I can't say the same about Riff Raff or Lil' Wayne, to whom my students have introduced me.

Macklemore's songs, however, lack a certain depth. Macklemore's songs are surfacey, resting on the same moral platitudes that many students have at the beginning of the semester of an Ethics 101 course: we all have our opinions, man, and you should respect them! His songs get abstractly preachy, but they do not bring you into their reality. You don't enter the Thug Life through them as you do with Tupac.

I have no idea who you are talking about, but I do like jazz.

THE ELDER

This type of analysis can extend far beyond the world of music. Within any realm, be it academic or cultural, the popular often mimics a deeper and more authentic struggle to which the popularizers give a mere lip-service, as Macklemore does with Tupac. I'm claiming the same here with science-worshiping atheism, either in the cartoonish or the tepid form. These folks aren't bad people; they're not Riff Raffs. They can just be preachy Macklemores, sharing the name "rap artist" with the Tupacs of the world. But they share in name only.

For those atheists who find themselves caught in the throes of science-worship, get rid of it. It doesn't stand. Give yourself over to the types of questions that lie at the heart of religiosity and atheism alike: questions concerning unnecessary suffering in the world; questions concerning the proliferation of violence over love. Here's where Tupac stands tall as opposed to Macklemore. He doesn't preach. He doesn't moralize. He merely offers concrete observations concerning how things seem really to work in this world: oftentimes like crap.

8

The Philosopher's Preference of PCs to Apple

A couple of years ago, I made a switch in the types of computers I used, contrary to this chapter's title. I moved from PC to Apple. I'm neither proud nor ashamed of this, and I admit to doing so only under some very, very specific conditions. I don't worship Apple products. They're nice, sure, but they're also *really* expensive, and you don't drive a Ferrari unless you can both afford it and use the power to squeal around a track. It turns out that both these conditions were met for me.

For one, someone else started buying my computers, namely, the institution that I work for. I was given the option between a MacBook and a PC laptop, and I decided to see what all the fuss was about on the Apple side of things. Second, I began doing a lot of videos for my classes, recording my lectures ahead of time. The smoothness of the Apple software under these circumstances made all the difference for me as opposed to the programs that I tried using on a PC. Thus I justified my switch. Apple software simply doesn't gum up the way it does on PCs.

The experience of trying to record, edit, and create a video on an Apple versus a PC made me into a bit of an Apple snob. The Apple platform is already centralized, and the software programs are pieced together with each other in mind. They communicate well with each other; they eventually communicate with the user (no, my friends, Apple's not as intuitive as you think unless you've used Apple for years); and they come on a quality piece of silver-encrusted hardware. They're a yuppie's delight!

I bring up this silly point because, frankly, it feels like we exist in the PC version of the world at times—the world feels buggy, thrown together, a series of ad hoc processes being tossed into one noncentralized platform. Like a PC, when you throw a bunch of parts and programs onto the same platform without any specific tuning, suffering is going to emerge. That suffering comes in the form of programs that can't communicate well with each other or that can't communicate well with the user, usually both.

In philosophy-of-religion circles, we not-so-creatively call these issues as we experience them in the broader world (and not just PCs) the problem of evil and the problem of suffering. The world seems gummed up and doesn't operate properly. There's too much wrong with it. Because it all seems a little out of whack, a lot of people get subjected to heinous and unnecessary suffering, and it feels like we can't justify belief in the existence of an all-powerful, all-good God in light of these issues. Either God in God's self is shady, or we live in a crap world where there exists no centralized Apple programmer.

The Apple logo is a once-bit apple . . .

THE DEACON

The Problem of Suffering and the Defense of PCs

In his *Black Dog of Fate: A Memoir*, Peter Balakian quotes a diplomat to Turkey in the late nineteenth century named Henry Morgenthau. Morgenthau writes about the Armenian genocide:

> The Central Government now announced its intentions of gathering the two million or more Armenians living in the several sections of the empire and transporting them to this desolate and inhospitable region. . . . The real purpose of the deportation was robbery and destruction; it really represented a new method of massacre. When the Turkish authorities gave the orders for these deportations, they were merely giving the death warrant to a whole race; they understood this well, and in their conversations with me they made no particular attempt to conceal the fact.[1]

He goes on to describe one of these marches.

> On the seventh day a few creatures reached Aleppo. Out of the consigned convoy of 18,000 souls just 150 women and children reached their destination. A few of the rest, the most attractive, were still living as captives of the Kurds and Turks; all the rest were dead.[2]

We can only surmise what was happening with this remnant of "the most attractive."

Take a look, too, at David E. Stannard's *American Holocaust: The Conquest of the New World*, where Stannard quotes a man named La Casas about the natives and their treatment by the Spaniards:

> [W]ithout any offense on their part, they were despoiled of their kingdoms, their lands and liberties, and their lives, their wives, and homes. As they saw themselves each day perishing by the cruel and inhuman treatment of the Spaniards, crushed to the earth by the horses, cut in pieces by swords, eaten and torn by dogs, many buried alive and suffering all kinds of exquisite tortures . . . [they] decided to abandon themselves to their unhappy fate with no further struggle, placing themselves in the hands of their enemies that they might do with them as they liked.[3]

It's difficult to imagine the duress you'd be under to eventually believe that giving yourself to a pack of wild dogs (and I'm not sure whether "wild dogs" refers to actual dogs or the Spanish conquerors) becomes your best option.

The idea of suffering can have many particular forms. We get thirsty, and we suffer in that. We get hungry, and we definitely suffer in that. We want to know the newest bands, and hipsters suffer when they don't know them. Or, more seriously, we may lose someone important, a sister, a father, and in this loss we suffer an unquenchable need to be with that person again, losing even a piece of our own identities in such suffering. I believe that's why you hear persons say after someone close to them dies, "I just want to feel myself again." Any which way you look at it, suffering in its basic structure simply stands for unquenched desire and, in this regard, the Buddha was correct: life is suffering. We always have unquenched desires.

The questions arising from evil and suffering are the main reason I see people walk away from God.

THE BISHOP

Still, I wouldn't say that every time I'm thirsty, something spiritually important is at stake, unless you count a strong desire for a Cabernet Sauvignon as important. When we're dealing with the problem of suffering philosophically, we're not merely dealing with having bad gas or even moving our way through important loss; we're dealing with issues in which a person's place in this world falls to a lesser state. We call this place "undignified" and, in it, a basic and primordial desire that we have to be seen for who we are—beloved and worthy of that love—comes to the fore and is at stake. In indignity, we're lowered, dejected, and accosted by someone or something that doesn't care who we are, and who refuses to acknowledge our God-breathed worth. We're made meaningless. That's why the atrocious stories above, aside even from the severe physical and psychological suffering involved, take on the tenor of horror stories. They deal with indignity.

To a *far* lesser degree, such indignity and suffering resulting from it shows up in everyday life as well. Do you treat your waitress or waiter as a person? Do you tell off your bank-teller? Do you work for the Department of Motor Vehicles and purposely make everyone's life a living hell? All of these exemplify small but real indignities that we can inflict on other, sometimes accidentally but too often purposely. While the degrees of such maltreatment are *almost* incomparable, suffering indignity still has that same basic shape wherever it's found, meaning we can call these lesser phenomena the seeds of the more serious, tyrannical kinds.

Real atheistic rejection begins to emerge in light of things like indignity, a form of suffering that in its most extreme cases serves no justifiable purposes. We cannot look at the Holocaust and take seriously the claim that, for instance, "God's punishing the Israelites for straying from covenant, just like when God punished the Israelites and sent them to Babylon." Most Jewish thinkers reject this absurd claim. Take my friend and colleague, Barry Ferst, who says "a number of those who were killed in these death camps were people who had given so much to European civilization. They were doctors and lawyers, persons whose goals were to give themselves to others. This would make God punish people for doing God's work."[4]

Jews not only did no wrong but were somehow punished for doing good in the world? No, when we look at the Holocaust, we are to look to and side with Job when, at the end of this book, he accuses God of treating him unfairly. God's only answer to Job is as follows: "Mr. Job, how can you know my purposes? Did *you* create the Leviathan?" That's an answer that I'd give to my daughter regarding why she can't ultimately shove raisins up her nose, but it doesn't help us with either Job's treatment or the Jews' suffering during the Holocaust. The Jews, like Job, seemed to have been crapped on for no good reason, and as you've seen, they're not the only peoples in history to have been treated in these undignified, even satanic ways!

We should see the clear path now regarding how suffering indignity—or any other seemingly pointless evil—unfolds into the question of the existence of God, or at least the worthiness of God to be worshiped. From a theistic perspective, we might say that God is all-good and benevolent, or that God is all-powerful, but the atheist points out that we cannot say that God is both in light of the undue suffering and indignity in the world. Atheistic

The problem of evil may not have a good answer, but if you don't take it seriously you aren't a thoughtful Christian.

THE ELDER

arguments based on the problem of undignified suffering are a direct challenge to the possibility of the essence and existence of God. I will confess that I've found no philosophical answer that has been satisfying because none can justify the torment that took place in the many holocausts of the past two centuries. But philosophy does provide some answers, and these answers are worth considering. I will only give a taste of how these arguments usually unfold, however, because I'm personally far more interested in getting completely beyond them.

The usual way of answering these types of questions pertains to what philosophers call a free will defense, which usually looks to argue in the following way. God, in fact, cannot do simply anything, and so cannot logically stop evil from emerging in a world that has freedom within it. Moreover, it's important that God creates a world with freedom in it so that, in this world, there do not exist merely automata (fleshy robots) but beings who can choose between good and evil. For this world to be truly good, God has to make beings that can freely choose his will or reject it, otherwise no one will choose goodness for its own sake and because of its inherent worth.

For the free will defense argument, when things don't work perfectly, it's not a matter of the platform maker messing things up or creating a poor platform. Rather, the emergence of evil and suffering stems from later software designers freely creating memory-hogging and incompatible programs, which bog everything down. For the free will defender, we must not blame God for this world's issues but must rather blame human creativity, which has control over the types of software developed in this world. By our rejection of what's "actually good" for "what's good for us," we bog this platform down, creating suffering.

If you delve into this literature, what you'll find is a never-ending movement of tit-for-tat arguments developed by atheists and theists. The basic gist of this exchange will look as follows: theists will defend the image of the PC world, and they'll have a number of logically viable answers for any of the concerns that the atheist has. The atheist will continue to argue for a different platform, that God could have gone Apple.

So, there ya go, I guess. Problem solved.

Protest Theism

I've worked a fair amount of construction during my life. One of the first places that I worked was a pretty big construction company in Seattle. I held the inglorious job of being a laborer, which means I got to clean up all the junk other, more skilled workers left lying around.

I was hired on to this company with the help of a friend's grandpa, who himself was a major player. I have to say, this friend's grandpa was an extremely kind man, always buying us meals and telling good stories about his homeland, Iceland. Because of him, I looked forward to this job, which was only reconfirmed when I interviewed with some nice folks in downtown Seattle and signed on. What a great opportunity!

The problem was that the people I worked with were not the people who hired me. They were veterans of the construction site itself, and they didn't have time for an inexperienced, naïve college student. They were jerks, to be honest, but I don't necessarily blame them. Union jobs in the construction field are difficult to come by, and these guys felt that I, a young kid in college with opportunities aplenty, was treading on their space, taking jobs from them and their kind. Still, they were unnecessarily angry, gave me extra work, and generally treated me like more of a piece of turd than I actually was. Not being terribly strong-willed at the time, I left the job midsummer as I had no desire to relive the young adult equivalent of junior high.

My point, here, is simple. While the people at the top of the company were very kind, the people I had to work with were not. When you have to deal with indignities on an everyday basis within a company, it doesn't matter if your boss's boss's boss is a cool person. You only know your boss, who smells like chaw and stale beer, and constantly belittles your manhood. The goodness, kindness, or generosity of the topmost people simply don't matter.

THE BISHOP

I imagine the pope has similar concerns.

Real suffering—suffering far beyond what I've ever experienced in these small slights—pervades this world. For those of us who haven't suffered greatly or even slightly, we will eventually feel its cold hand. We will all lose loved ones; we will all get sick; we will all lose bodily function as we age; we will be told by someone, purposefully or not, that we're not worth the cost of the skin we're put in. We will know these forms of suffering soon enough.

Because of suffering, we find a "so what?" factor. So we have a God at the top of all things who's perfect, experiences no suffering, and is an all-around swell guy. Well, just as I didn't deal with my boss's boss's boss except during the interview, I don't have to deal with this God on an everyday basis; I have to deal with a bunch of jerks who're more interested in hazing me than working. That is, I have to deal with this world and the experience of suffering in it. Someone in this position shouldn't care about the boss's boss's boss.

While I still believe that we can't get around Miyagi intellectually, I've also come to believe that such a God certainly doesn't matter much for us without something more, without a "so what?" factor to incorporate. I've already brought this point up in the third chapter, and I'm coming back to it. A famous philosopher named Martin Heidegger makes a statement that has become rather commonplace. Miyagi-God doesn't give us anything to worship, and worship is ultimately what we seek in our gods! I used to get frustrated with this critique because people seemed to want to use it to deny, by a rhetorical sleight of hand, the possibility of Miyagi-God. While I think most people use the phrase in just that way, I've come to get the statement Heidegger's making. What I now take him to be saying is that a God who sits on high, far above the fray of this world and its absurdities, just isn't worth thinking about, even if that God is logically consistent with the world as we experience it.

Rarely do we deal with Miyagi-God in any explicitly important matters in our everyday living. Miyagi doesn't seem to affect the one thing that grips us most: our suffering in the world. If Miyagi, the philosopher's God, is the only one to which we look for hope or inspiration, we become effectively atheistic even while acknowledging this God's existence. Sure, we can admit to the reality of such a divinity, but we also have no real reason beyond the intellectual to care!

That's the "so what?" factor. The atheist says, "So what if this philosopher's God exists? It does nothing about the issue and problem that affects us most: suffering." The atheist is correct in this regard. This God has somehow allowed for a pile of Chinese citizens' heads to be amassed and neatly stacked, cut off as sport for Japanese soldiers after the invasion of Nanking in 1937.[5] This God has allowed for medical experimentation on Jewish children during the Nazi regime's attempts to rid itself of what it considered a problem-people.[6] Are these answers worth freedom, the ability to accept or reject God noncompulsorily?

To this critique, a purely philosophical answer—really any answer—always falls short. In light of the above philosophical possibilities, I must confess that I'd simply give myself over to protest theism: that, although I must acknowledge the existence of God, I wish I didn't have to; that I don't think free will is worth it; that I'd give up all the freedom in the world to prevent these things from happening; and that I don't believe a good God should allow for these things to happen either.

In a world filled with real tragedy and real suffering, few people care if a God like Miyagi exists, even if it can be made intellectually consistent with the problem of evil and suffering. Only a couple of intellectuals care. The rest conclude that such a God isn't worth thinking about too much. After all, we've got the next genocide to try to prevent, and we don't have time to waste given God's seeming lack of worldly concern.

God Did Not Look
Like a Norwegian Hippie

We now face what I'm calling the "so what?" of the philosopher's God: we've got to find an answer for the viability of the philosopher's God, Miyagi, as something worth caring about in the first place! The task isn't an easy one, and I don't think I'll convince anyone that we should care for this God unless we jump past the standpoint of presumably pure reason and into the realm of what we call faith. We've got to move beyond the God of the philosophers and into the biblical God; we need to move from the God of reason to the God of relation. After all, when we Catholics gather together for the mass, or when Methodists gather for a worship service, we're not gathering out of some metaphysical desire to affirm Miyagi. God means something beyond a principle.

On Gods and Voltron

Voltron is easily the coolest cartoon that many of you are probably way too young to know. I watched it as a child, and I begged my parents for the action figures. Voltron was the name of a massive, evil-fighting, sword-wielding robot, and he fights his enemies in space. Space! That's how cool Voltron is: he battles space-evil with a massive robotic sword to create lion-based, intergalactic peace. Yes, I said lion-based.

THE DEACON

You must not have a young boy yet, because Netflix rebooted Voltron and it is back! The only problem is when the lions get together the leader says, "Form Voltron."

You see, Voltron was made up of five gigantic robot lions. These lions were controlled by human operators who dedicated themselves to biting injustice in the face with massive, mechanized mandibles. When those mandibles weren't strong enough on their own, that's when they'd team up to form the even more powerful Voltron, two lions becoming the legs, two lions becoming the arms, and one forming the torso and head.

Voltron is a lot like Captain Planet, only without as many mullets and without an explicitly anti-radiation message.

The Christian faith has, from a very early point in its history, existed in a Voltron-esque tension somewhere between the God of the philosophers like Miyagi and the biblical God. Like the Greek philosophers who first developed the idea of Miyagi, many early Christian thinkers were unwilling to portray their God like a shredded Old-Man River, aka Zeus. No, truth had to be involved with God, and truth emerges in and through reason. The early church made a decision for truth.[1]

Miyagi's importance continued to affect early Christians. Still, these theologians couldn't ignore the experience of the God whom they discovered, whose claim to fame came through the crazy story of a supposedly resurrected Jew named Jesus. They couldn't ignore a God who, through a sense of relationship and a promise of salvation, gave them the capacity to answer the "so what?" problem that emerges in light of the world's suffering.

Just as the lions of Voltron come together to create an awesome, sword-wielding, forty-story-tall robot, it became the job of the Christian theologians to bring these two visions of God together and pair them into an even *mightier* God: the truth of the impersonal Miyagi meets the utterly salvific, interpersonal interpretation of God through Christ.

I believe that this job remains today for those of us who buy into the Christian vision of God and God's salvation, and if we can find a way to make this God fight injustice in space with a cosmic sword, even better! At the very least, we'll find a possible answer to the atheist's properly posed "so what?" question.

God Was Not a Norwegian Hippie

When I say the name Jesus, we have the same image issue that we had with our concept of God. We envision Jesus as a Norwegian Hippie, just like we thought of God as a shredded Old-Man River. This vision of Jesus leads us astray, killing a proper interpretation of who Jesus was and what he means to God. The Norwegian Hippie Jesus is the blonde-haired, blue-eyed pretty boy we've come to know in a number of incarnations: a man walking through a pasture with a lamb over his shoulders; a man sitting on a tree stump with a child on a knee; or a man looking tenderly to heaven while nailed nigh bloodlessly to a Roman death device called a cross.

THE ELDER

The problem today is that the blue-eyed stud of a Jesus painting in every church has some serious competition every time someone makes a Jesus movie. He keeps getting better looking.

In fact, this Norwegian Hippie Jesus is an Aryan self-help master who reminds me a lot of Michael Myers's character *The Love Guru*. He'll teach us the key principles to happiness in this world, even if with one minor correction to Myers's overly randy spiritual leader. For the liberal hippie Jesus, these keys to happiness usually mean being kind to strangers and refusing to judge others. For the more conservative version, the keys are learning how not to lust too much, and learning how to "let go and let God." Or, if you're into the prosperity gospel, he'll also teach you the principles for getting rich, which just straight-up buys you happiness!

Other than the prosperity gospel, both the liberal and conservative Jesuses have some very important points, and I'm not rejecting portions of what comes from them. Being nice to strangers *is* good, and learning that you are not your own source of life is extremely important, too. Both ethical modes of thinking are, in fact, important to the Christian faith. The problem is this: these interpretations of Jesus have been separated from Jesus's actual story and have been turned into spiritual principles that are keys to gaining some kind of spiritual happiness. Since doughnuts also make us happy, we can call these lessons spiritual doughnuts, and I'm just not sure Jesus cares first and foremost about spiritual doughnuts. After all, rather than being particularly happy, Jesus was in despair, crying out at the end of his life, "My God, My God, why have you forsaken me?"

I dough-nut know, I am
pretty sure every spiritual
lesson has a hole in the
center without Jesus.
(still joking.)

THE DEACON

The point is that we need to reinterpret our Norwegian Hippie in terms of what he actually was: a radical Jewish prophet. As a prophet, his ministry seems caught up in an utter adoration for, and dedication to, divine peace. In this divine peace, we can find the seeds of God's better answer to the problem of suffering than those philosophical answers given. Salvation is salvation from indignity, suffering, despair, and the violence of death that undergirds it all; salvation is salvation as oriented toward this divine peace.

I want to call divine peace by its original name: *shalom*. Genesis metaphorically describes the concept through the garden of Eden: God, persons, beasts, and creation in their entirety live in an utter, loving wholeness with another. There exists no violence and no disorder, and there seems to be no will to dominate other persons, creatures, or God. There merely exists divine peace, which God creates, observes on the seventh day, and calls good.

But it's not just the creation stories that conjure this idea of divine peace. The loss of this mythical land called Eden also elicits a sense of shalom indirectly. Sin is portrayed as a disturbance of this shalom, the original disturbance manifesting itself in the whole of creation and creating what we've come to call doctrinally "original sin." A good chunk of the redemption narrative seems filled with God either trying to save creation from this disruption of shalom, or giving those who've disrupted it over to that disruption.

For instance, Noah's not just some crazy story about a weirdo building a big boat. The story is about God giving up on a violent and fallen creation that has turned away from God's orderly creation. God is trying to start anew.

The flood language in the Noah story exactly mimics the creation language in the first creation story but in an opposite way. Instead of separating the waters, night and day, dry land from sea, God allows all these good, shalomy things to be swallowed once more into the chaotic waters of the deep. God starts creation anew.

Or look at Sodom and Gomorrah, which have become synonymous with a misguided idea of God's hatred for gay folks. Look at the story again and what it condemns. Two angels come into town and, in the spirit of generosity, Lot invites them to stay in his home. They eventually agree to come in with Lot, and then crowds congregate outside Lot's home asking to "know" the men. That's Bible code for sex, in this case rape. Lot, refusing to let the folks outside have their way with the Angel-men, offers them his daughters instead. That's right! Lot simply offers up his daughters to be "known" by the folks outside, presumably like any good father. The angelic strangers are sickened by this act, blind the crowd, and tell Lot that the city will be destroyed. Like

---

I don't know which is a bigger surprise, the sin of Sodom wasn't about homosexuality or that after that move Lot is allowed to get out alive.

THE BISHOP

---

the flood, wickedness, violence, and the rejection of shalom have taken hold. Sodom is an extremely rape-friendly place, filled with chaos and disorder, and God hands Sodom and Gomorrah back over to the chaos of destruction just like God did with the earth prior to Noah.

Shalom is key in all biblical texts for understanding the salvation story because salvation is ultimately a re-creation of shalom and salvation from the indignities of unjustifiable suffering.

He's Bringing Shalom Back

We now all know that the good Mr. Justin Timberlake has, with his slick dance moves, daring falsetto, and overall SNL hilariousness, brought sexy back. He's said so himself, and he's right. Little did you know, however, that Jesus's ministry was similarly bringing shalom back, which I'm assuming had little to do with songs about friends' mothers and more to do with healing mothers' dead children. If we want to understand Jesus beyond Norwegian Hippie categories, we're going to have to see how Jesus brings shalom back.

The Gospel of Matthew presents a picture of Jesus that is more in sync (see what I did there?) with the Old Testament than any other Gospel. Jesus is introduced via a genealogy, which isn't all that interesting to read but is very important. The genealogy shows that Jesus is the king of Israel, of the line of Israel's most famous king, David, the messiah. He's also the fulcrum of the relationship between God and Israel, bringing together the promises that God made to all the important patriarchs like Noah and Abraham and all those who are less than pure, like Rahab, the prostitute. Jesus is presented as the one who Isaiah promises will restore justice and peace, the new

I know it isn't a big deal to you, but the first time you realize the character of "God" in the Bible doesn't always fully correspond to God (as God really is to God) then the Bible isn't nearly as embarrassing.

THE ACOLYTE

shoot who comes from the stump of Jesse (David's father), and the branch emerging from the roots of a seemingly dead Israel.[2] Salvific overtones flow forth from all sides of the introduction.

Matthew then discusses something extremely important and a lot more interesting than the genealogy. Jesus relives the whole history of Israel as if to prove what was said through the genealogy: Jesus is the God-anointed king and representative of Israel. Look at the parallels between Jesus's life and Israel's history. First, Herod, hearing of this newborn king, begins slaughtering newborn males, confirming that ancient kings really sucked. This act is emblematic of the Pharaoh's intention in Exodus to slaughter the infant male Hebrews, from which Moses, the future leader of Israel, escapes. Jesus is likened to the new Moses. We then have Jesus's escape to and back from Egypt, which was the experience of the Israelites. Jesus is baptized by John, just as the Israelites had to escape across the Red Sea and just as they entered, with Joshua (which is actually Jesus's name), the promised land through the Jordan. And then Jesus spends forty days and forty nights in the desert being tempted, just as the Israelites spent forty years in the desert. Finally, Jesus introduces his full-fledged ministry with the Sermon on the Mount, which refers back to Moses' sermon to the Israelites as they look into the promised land of Canaan. Jesus is Israel, personified.

But Matthew seems insistent on differentiating one thing. Where the Israelites failed, Jesus succeeds. Where the Israelites complained in the desert, Jesus rebukes Satan and resists temptation. Where the Israelites charged into the promised land, swords clanking, Jesus commands his followers in the Sermon on the Mount to turn the other cheek, go the extra mile, and take up the cross.

Jesus's ministry seems, for Matthew, to be a correction of the way Israel had thought it was supposed to be Israel: as a kingdom that oppresses its enemies in the way that Rome and Babylon did, by way of force and violence. Matthew sees that such a kingdom is no different than the violent Roman and Babylonian kingdoms, and that the Israelites who claim to serve the God of all nations make a claim no different than any other kingdom; their God or gods empower them to defeat all other peoples, thus showing this God's worth. Rather, Jesus demonstrates what it really means for his people, Israel, to be the beacon upon the hill and the salt of the earth. They were supposed to have been the lovers of peace, the suffering servants, the ones who brought the image of God to the world in shalom; instead they brought as much violence and destruction as their pagan neighbors.

If we are to understand Jesus for who he was, we must see that he was subverting his people's self-interpretation and what they expected from their king.[3] You see, we find the emblem for what kingship means to Israel through David, and he was *extremely* violent. In fact, in 1 Chronicles 22:8, God rebuffs David, who wants to build God a temple, telling David that he'll not be the one to build God a temple because "you have shed much blood on the earth in My sight," which is an understatement given the number of dismembered foreskins alone David presents to his forebear, Saul, as a dowry.[4] Solomon presumably becomes the one to build God's temple in David's stead because he'll rule not with the sword but with wisdom. But Matthew's claim is that it's not Solomon but Jesus, a distant descendant of David, who truly understands the temple and has the rights to build it. This is exactly what Jesus does.

The radical Jewish prophet Jesus actively rebuilds the temple by entering the sacred space near the end of his life, taking it over from the money-changers and cultic officials. He drives these persons out and shows what the temple was supposed to be doing all along: not selling doves to sacrifice and certainly not acting as a device for the ruling elite to actively oppress the people of Israel. It was supposed to be a place of healing, of bringing about the shalom that rightly reflects God. So, Matthew, with a tone that sees the next act of Jesus as the obvious conclusion to his temple antics, says, "[t]he blind and the lame came to him in the temple, and he cured them."[5]

To move this story along, it's subsequently these actions in the temple—where Jesus comes clean about his Davidic heritage and authority over the temple to Israel's authorities—that gets him killed. Only the Davidic king can make claims about the meaning of the temple, and Jesus makes exactly such claims in overturning the money-changers' tables. He's now a political threat to both Israel and Rome, making a treasonous claim to be the real king of Israel against Herod and Caesar's henchman in Pilate. The ruling class takes Jesus to be like the other revolutionaries around Jesus's time who will try to overthrow Roman rule, and, frankly, get Israel besieged by its antsy Roman overlords, which is exactly what happens in 70 CE. Understandably, for these authorities, Jesus must be stopped.

Of course, treason per se wasn't Jesus's purpose. He wanted to set Israel free from its misdiagnosis. But through Rome's and Israel's misinterpretations of him, he is labeled treasonous, which will lead to a confrontation between him and the very powers of violence and death themselves represented by Roman rule, and it's a battle that Jesus seems to lose given the fact that he's tossed up onto a humiliating Roman death device. But "lose" is the wrong term to use; it's not how a Christian interprets the cross. Certainly, Jesus's victory doesn't come by way of a heroic and *Iliad*-inspired ability to conquer his enemies. He rejects that victory in Gethsemane when he assures his disciples that he could have legions of angels come and destroy his arresters.[6] His victory comes only in weakness, by submitting himself to these powers and allowing them to have their way. The question is how we might count this as victory.

What a Radical Jewish Prophet Tells Us about God

In Jesus, we're not merely dealing with a man, according to the Christian tradition. The early church came to see this man as divine, and the divinity of Christ is necessary for the story to make any sense. When we say that Christ is divine, we affirm that what we say about him, we can also

> The power of God revealed on Golgotha is a cross-bearing one and not a cross-building one.

THE DEACON

say about God the Father. If Christ loves us, God loves us. If Christ hates us, God hates us. If Christ offers a slice of barbecue chicken pizza, you can rest assured that it's of the divine and will be the tastiest you'll ever have.

According to this logic, Christ's miracles directly express the salvation of God. Christ, for instance, restores sick persons' bodies to their proper forms, curing them of their ailments. He also heals these same people's social rejection, making them whole again by reestablishing their graceful place within the community of God's people, Israel, whose head is now found not in the temple authorities or Herod but Jesus himself. It's no different with the prostitutes or tax-collectors: all are healed even when no cure is needed. All are welcomed back into God's community, told to "[g]o your way, and from now on do not sin again."[7]

Even still, Jesus brings the peace of healing to nature itself, calming the same chaotic flood waters of Noah that begin to bubble beneath his and his disciples' boat in the sea of Galilee.[8] The Lord of creation returns and calms the very same sea from which creation itself emerged, calling his creation back to its original, benign, and shalomic state. No part of creation will go unhealed.

More than anything, this logic of Jesus's divinity means that God does not abandon Jesus on the cross

THE ELDER

I tend to assume things can't change much and try to avoid being challenged by the level of change, healing, and transformation that characterized Jesus's ministry. I have lowered liberal expectations.

where Jesus confronts sin and death. Contrary to the standard divine-child-abuse models of the cross and salvation, the Christian faith has more traditionally thought of the cross as the centerpiece of God's confrontation with evil. It stands for a confrontation where the man, Jesus, does not merely call into question the political powers that be, Rome and its puppets in Judea; rather, Jesus confronts violence itself through these powers and the end toward which all violence flows, the nothing—death—which *The NeverEnding Story* so astutely interprets.[9]

In *The NeverEnding Story*, which can just as easily be titled *The NeverEnding Cavalcade of Awesome Names*, a young man and one of the main protagonists, Atreyu, is tasked by an empress with finding a way to stop the onslaught of a deep and dark storm-cloud called the Nothing from consuming her fantasy kingdom named, well, Fantasia. Gmork, a horrendously frightening and violent, wolf-like creature, is sent by the Nothing to stop Atreyu. Purposefully or not, in *The NeverEnding Story* there's at least an implied connection between the violence of Gmork and its only possible end: death, decay, and a fall into the storm-cloud of nothingness. Violence and nothingness become intimately intertwined through this movie such that there is no nothingness without violence or violence without nothingness.

Did you finish *The NeverEnding Story?* #trickquestion #neversaynever

THE ACOLYTE

Jesus cannot stop violence and its undertow into death with violence and expect to remain within the divine will, of which shalom, not war, is a direct reflection. That's simply contradictory. Moreover, a victory over death and violence by way of violence—the trampling of one's enemy—merely reestablishes the power of violence as that through which the world is ruled and will always be ruled. No, to find victory for Jesus is, paradoxically, for him to *submit* to violence. By way of the principle of what-we-say-about-Jesus-we-can-also-say-about-God, the cross comes to represent a place where the Lord of creation, through the man Jesus, refuses to fight the powers of violence and their undertow into nothingness in their own terms: through death, destruction, and violent interaction. In this refusal, the seeds are set for their strange demise.

Some of the church fathers understood this notion of atonement under the idea of "ransom," as God "buying back" God's creation from Satan, who is indistinguishable from the chaos and violence at the fore. Part of the ancient theory supposed that God, in becoming fully human, tricks the devil into taking a ransom payment that Satan will not have the power to keep: the divine in itself, disguised in human nature. This idea is fraught with difficulty, but I think it has some potential for how we might interpret God's actions on the cross.

To understand this ransom in its fullness, we need to draw loosely on a twentieth-century theologian with a magnificently German name, Eberhard Jüngel. Through him, we can maybe see how God finds victory over death without using the violent powers of death. On the cross, and in this moment where God gives himself over to the powers of sin and destruction, the nothing metaphorically thinks it has overtaken the divine that opposes its onslaught, be it through Rome, Babylon, Jerusalem, or Ebola. But God, instead, tricks the violence of nothingness, entering into it through his death on the cross and, in a reversal, incorporating the powers of death into God's own being in a new, creative, and ultimately nonviolent and salvific way. Jüngel calls this incorporation of nothingness into the being of God the Trinity.

Here's what I mean.

First off, the Trinity is *the* expression of love, so we can begin the question of the Trinity by discussing the nature of love. While love is complicated, we can bring some clarity to the concept by stating, first, that it's not a feeling. As a quick example, I loved my first daughter for the first six weeks of her life, but I didn't like her. I mean that. Infants are kind of jerks, and while I'd have given my life for her in half a second, I didn't want to hang out with her—a point that has more than happily changed in me since her infancy. Love is a commitment and a willed action rather than a brute emotion.

Second, love is an identity, which means that love transforms the person who we are and want to become through a relationship. Take marital love as an example. In marital love, you don't promise to retain your own individuality in union with another, as many marital partners promise to do in their vows to one another today. (That's a self-critique, by the way. There was a time when I would have affirmed this individuality, too.) To love your spouse is to receive your identity from your spouse, finding that you cannot be who you are any longer without your spouse to give your identity back in love. In a good marriage, this exchange of identities constitutes a two-way street such that your beloved also only receives who she is through you. What you strangely find is that, in this exchange, your identity is really you but found only in the identity of the one you love. You can't be yourself without the other whom you love.

I find it odd when someone insists they need more specific conclusions about God than their lifelong partner.

THE BISHOP

Another way to make this claim is to say that, in marital love, the ideas and relations into which I invest myself—my cares—are not merely mine anymore but mediated by another whom, in the best of times, I care for more than myself. My partner's cares are my utmost concern. I don't do what I want when I want but I give myself to her in order to form a collaborative journey. We then both have an obligation to form together better cares with one another out of the caring relationship that's formed between us, such as those cares found in, for instance, having children. Either way, identity and care depend on another in marital forms of love.[10]

Here's where the theology kicks in. Just as we can talk about marital love in this manner, we can also talk about the Trinity in this way. In classical doctrines of the Trinity, each member of the Trinity exists in relationship to the others in such a manner that each member couldn't individually exist on their own. The Father cannot exist without the Son or Spirit. Same with the Son regarding the Spirit and Father, and with the Spirit regarding the Father and Son. Each person is relationally defined by the other. More importantly, this relationality means that each member of the Trinity actively gives itself over to each other member of the Trinity, receiving itself back in the process. In this giving and receiving, we see the real presence of love in the Trinity: that each member depends on the others in order to be, receiving themselves from the other.

In this interplay of identity through love, we should pay attention to a strange experience, at least when we experience love at its best. In love, we experience death, and I mean a real death. This death is not a physical death. It comes in the form of the death of an identity, the death of a self, which I believe is far more profound than any physical death we'll ever experience. By giving up myself in love, I die to myself, finding myself only in my beloved.

I find that I cannot be who I am without the beloved who loves me in return, and that's beautiful.

This love further reflects the Trinity and, in Christian terms, the salvation being offered on the cross. The Trinity is love and is even more so the self-sacrificial love that grounds, say, any marriage, or really any good and loving relationship. The members of the Trinity, in giving themselves to one another and receiving themselves back from one another, really and truly die to themselves in the process. They exist as nothing in themselves, and must receive themselves from each other in order to be who they are. This death does not simply mean that each member no longer exists but that they exist in the constancy of eternally dying to one another so as to receive themselves.

I forget how pretty the Trinity sounds in the mouth of someone who really cares.

THE DEACON

Death truly resides within the being of God. Unlike the power of death and destruction that we experience, which has the power to not only drag us into our mortal demise but unleash a cavalcade of indignities upon us in the process, death in God no longer has any power unto itself. It does not, so to say, "kill," but is creatively redirected through the power of the resurrection. God has reworked death so that it no longer poses a threat, and I'm not just talking psychologically here. Death does not extinguish life and its goodness, but it comes to express the relationship between things, and the fullness of what it means to exist through the real death we experience in loving and giving ourselves to one another. The difference is that, in this self-giving, we don't lose our lives and dignity as a rabbit loses its life in giving itself to the coyote for the coyote's sustenance. That represents the very notion of death that's overcome! We instead gain ourselves because our self is only possible in the presence of the other to whom we die in love.

God has ransomed us and our fall into death, and God has even maybe saved death itself from itself. God has reincorporated death and violence into the very being of God as Trinity, who lives, dies, and resurrects to itself eternally.

The cross, in this case, doesn't merely expose suffering and the violence that accompanies it; it doesn't merely gain our trust in God's willingness to suffer with us. The cross is that centerpiece from which, for all eternity, God turns the power of death found in destructive violence on its head. The cross is the point where God, as expressed in the eternality and life of the Trinitarian relations, repurposes the undertow of death into the backbone of relational being. God defeats destructive violence not with more violence but by way of a creative capacity to repurpose this previous parasite on existence into the foundation of existence.

God has also already achieved and completed all these things. Because God's life is eternal, God has always been the God who has come to us on the cross, who has always already worked out the undertow of nothingness and its violent submission of God's good created order. Creation and salvation remain inseparable. This eternality of God,

If the cross plays this big a role, wouldn't it or the Trinity be in earlier chapters? Is it normal to start talking about God's existence, essence, and historical situation before asking how the cross of Jesus shapes the situation?

THE ACOLYTE

however, touches us in time, in Christ, on the cross, and in the resurrection. We—this cosmos—are now the dough and God's salvation is the yeast, such that this yeast must and will work itself through the dough that is this world in time as it already has been completed from the standpoint of eternity.

Conclusion

In returning to the wondrous cartoon *Voltron*, you can see that we face two very distinct ideas of God, and they don't easily unite. One is Miyagi-God, who sits both above and within all things, feeding them life-giving identity but taking no active part in their existence. The other is our Hippie Aunt-God and Joan of Arc-God, who enter conscientiously into the very fabric of human existence, calling it back to what it was supposed to be and giving of herself for the salvation of all things that are threatened by violence, death, and destruction. One is a God about whom we care intellectually, who grounds the pursuit of Truth. The others are Gods whom we can trust, and who concretely address the atheist's question, "so what?" The one has to be made consistent with the problem of evil, coming up with reasons why they are compatible. The others remain entirely inconsistent with the problem of evil, unsatisfied with its continued proliferation in the very cosmos to which this God has given herself to stop it.

These Gods come together in the Christian mind, and they form a more formidable, cosmic, lion-shaped robot. They come together in the fact that we Christians now see relationality *within* the rationally undeniable existence of

Miyagi. We reinterpret Miyagi according to the atheist's "so-what?," no longer accepting the stand-offish terms of the philosophers but seeing God now within the context of a history of salvation culminating in Christ. We now understand God not only as a ground of all identity but also as the caring call of creation by our Hippie Aunt back to its best possibilities, the likes of which emerge in the selfishness-busting, loving powers of Joan of Arc. We come to see in Miyagi not distance but what Paul calls *kenosis*, which is a fancy Greek term for self-emptying, and what I've been calling love. God is the scandalous one who comes not in military might but in the poverty of an oppressed Galilean; the Lord comes not in the victory of power but the subversion of the cross.

God is the cosmic centerpiece who need not come, probably shouldn't come, but does come nonetheless, and Christians claim to be able to make this move, maybe unacceptably, because of both their experience of Christ and because of God's very self-revelation as this Christ through Joan of Arc. So we're led back to Pope Benedict when he writes,

> This God who had previously existed as something neutral, as the highest, culminating concept; this God who had been understood as pure Being or pure thought, circling around forever closed in upon itself without reaching over to man and his little world; this God of the philosophers, whose pure eternity and unchangeability had excluded any relation with the changeable and transitory, now appeared to the eye of faith as the God of men, who is not only the thought of all thoughts, the eternal mathematics of the universe, but also *agape*, the power of creative love.[1]

The question is whether we Christians are actually *allowed* to make this bold move of reinterpreting god into creative love.

I think your Hippie
Aunt would volunteer
to help.   **THE DEACON**

Certainly the move isn't based on some notion of pure reason, as if we could deduce these actions of God based on Miyagi's definition. After all, we're affirming what seems at first to be the most unreasonable of conclusions: that out of the billions of galaxies, God actually cared enough to come to our little Milky Way, in our insubstantial solar system, to our small planet in the form of a peasant, first-century Jew. We're claiming that this presumed Jewish carpenter is important to the trajectory of the universe, which is as unreasonable a claim as we can make up.

Not all is lost at the level of reason, however.

Augustine has a wonderful passage in his most famous book, *Confessions*, where in throes of the question of who God is and where to find God, he asks:

> And what is the object of my love? I asked the earth and it said: "it is not I." I asked all that is in it; they made the same confession. I asked the sea, the deeps, the living creatures that creep, and they responded: "We are not your God, look beyond us." I asked the breezes which blow and the entire air with its inhabitants said: "Anax-imenes was mistaken; I am not God." I asked

heaven, sun, moon, and stars; they said: "Nor are we the God whom you seek." And I said to all these things in my external environment: "Tell me of my God who you are not, tell me something about him." And with a great voice they cried out: "He made us." My question was the attention I gave to them and their response was their beauty.[2]

That Augustine proclaims the beauty of creation to attest to the truth of the divine is of great importance.

Go for a hike sometime up a mountainside. When you reach the peak of the mountain, stop, take a look around you, and sit for a few minutes. Pay attention to yourself in the moment that you take in the beauty of the valley into which you look, or the next mountain peak onto which you gaze. Or, frankly, listen to a beautiful piece of music. Symphonies lend themselves to beauty, as does Duke Ellington, and so does the wonderfully strange '80s pop-rocker, Peter Gabriel. When you're caught up in the pulse of music or the beauty of the landscape, your world is opened, and you're faced with new possibilities for how you understand yourself in relationship to the world. The world no longer exists for us, but we're given over to the objects of the world for their own sake, as important beyond what we want of them. Beauty opens us to a world beyond ourselves.

With this point in mind, look now to truth. Augustine again says,

I turned then to examine the nature of the mind, but false opinion which I held about [intellectual] entities did not allow me to perceive the truth.

The truth with great force leapt to my eyes, but I used to turn away my agitated mind from incorporeal reality to lines and colours and physical magnitudes of great size. . . . My opinion was miserable folly.[3]

On the one hand, we like to talk about truth as common sense, but Augustine is clear: his commonsense opinion was miserable folly. Common sense is oftentimes common nonsense, and our commonsense ways of viewing the world have more to do with enculturation than with truth. Common sense most certainly concerns itself more with ease of thought than with a willingness to wonder and explore. Like Callicles in relationship to Socrates, it's concerned with holding onto what it thinks it already knows rather than taking up what it should know.

On the other hand, real truth is that which pulls us away from what we're told is the case, what we want to believe is the case, and what our finite natures naturally incline us to think is the case. Truth and our desire for it beckon us beyond the commonsense world as we're used to interpreting it unto a world as it is, breaking our interpretations apart in the process.

It's reasonable to notice here that beauty functions very similarly to truth in the fullest and deepest sense of the term. After all, truth never merely affirms our commonsense ways of seeing the world; it opens us to the reality of the world. Neither does beauty simply allow us to interact with the world in our commonsense, selfish ways; it attunes us unselfishly to care for things in our world rather than merely ourselves.

I note this relation because in the deepest of Western philosophical traditions, truth, beauty, goodness, being, oneness—all of these simply function as different sides of the same multifaceted dice that is Miyagi-God. God is the Beautiful just as God is the Good and the True. More precisely, God is the act of Beauty that allows for all good things to be illumined and seen; God is the Good that all things seek and in whom all things find their meaning; God is also the One who knows the real order of the world and thus the Truth, and in Christian terms is calling this world back to the way it's supposed to be in Christ.

Beauty is indistinct from Miyagi-God, the very ground of reason, and the one who beckons us beyond ourselves and our small worlds. We Christians maybe—just *maybe*—reserve the right to see the Good news of Christ in this vein of beauty. Of course, maybe the Christian faith is a bad LSD trip, a product of wishful thinking that truth needs to overcome, but, with Luther, I say "Here I stand; I can do no other." I'm simply given over to the beauty of the Gospel, even if I can never fully justify the Good News that God, in Christ, has come to save us from the undignified and prolific sufferings of this world.

So, while we can see that these statements about God's coming to us seem absurd, they also draw us into the beauty of hope. In their shocking disregard for how we're told the world must be, and their scandalous proclamation that God has come, they most certainly call us away from a world that we thought we knew, exposing a functional identity between beauty and truth. To the degree that truth functions similarly to beauty, we hold out hope that, in the Spirit, the two will ultimately become united: that the beauty of God's coming to us in the peace of Christ also represents God's truly coming.

Notes

Chapter 1

1. Pope Benedict, *Introduction to Christianity* (San Francisco: Ignatius, 2004), 143. So-called conservative Catholics so often get thrown under the bus as having only a naïve conception of the classical concept of God at their disposal. As you can see, the truth is *far* from the common assumption—just as the truth often is.

Chapter 2

1. Exodus 3:13–15, NRSV.
2. Acts 17:28.
3. Judges 11:34–35, NRSV.
4. Genesis 2:1–3, NRSV.
5. Peter Beinart, "Jeb Bush Tries to Push the Pope out of Politics," *The Atlantic*, June 17, 2015, http://www.theatlantic.com/politics/archive/2015/06/jeb-bush-catholicism-climate-change/396158/ accessed January 26, 2016.

Chapter 3

1. *I'm Sorry You Feel That Way*, directed by Jay Karas (Atlanta: New Entertainment Television, 2014).
2. 1 John 1:14.
3. 1 Corinthians 1:18-19, 25.
4. Plato, *Meno* (Indianapolis: Hackett, 2002), 80d.

Chapter 4

1. John B. Cobb Jr. and David Ray Griffin, *Process Theology: An Introductory Exposition* (Louisville: Westminster John Knox, 1976), 14.

2. St. Thomas more or less writes the basis of Catholic theology after him. Anything that you think of that's particularly Catholic likely emerges with Thomas and his creative genius, which you'd likely know if only you'd stop listening to Tripp Fuller and start reading the *Summa Theologica*. In all seriousness, Aquinas is extremely important and is sometimes taken too seriously in my circles, as I believe that truth is never simply grasped by one thinker alone but in a community, including the living and the dead, of thinkers in dialogue.

3. St. Thomas Aquinas, *Summa Theologiae: A Concise Translation*, ed. Timothy McDermott (Notre Dame: Ave Maria, 1989), 38.

Chapter 5

1. "Priest Religious but Not Really Spiritual," *The Onion*, Vol. 46, issue 18, May 5, 2010, accessed May 3, 2016: http://www.theonion .com/article/priest-religious-but-not-really-spiritual-17373.

2. Amos 9:13.

3. Mechthild of Magdeburg, *The Flowing Light of the Godhead*, trans. Frank Tobin (Mahwah, NJ: Paulist, 1998), 62.

Chapter 6

1. I think it's funny that the least accepting tradition of anything postmodern, the Catholic, has always gotten this one correct. We don't cover up who we disagree with for the sake of convenience. That's important. It allows Catholics to talk to others as Catholics and nothing less, only becoming a problem when the difference is used to wedgie the conversation partner into becoming Catholic.

2. I'm going to be honest, here. This quote is an internet quote that I can't find in a real book. MSN put it up (http://www .msn.com/en-us/news/world/the-14th-dalai-lama-at-80-a-life -in-quotes/ss-AAclCx8#image=14, accessed May 20, 2016), which means that I can give it around a 50 percent chance of being something that came out of the Dalai Lama's mouth. Even with only this 50 percent chance, persons will much more readily listen to a Dalai Lama-esque statement than a jerk Catholic about interreligious dialogue.

Chapter 7

1. Plato, *Gorgias* (Indianapolis: Hackett, 1987), 513c.

2. Catholics aren't afraid of history, and we're especially not afraid of looking old-fashioned. That's why we know that these empiricist ideas of truth are named after an ancient Greek philosopher: Sextus Empiricus. He, however, didn't argue for the eternal values of the sciences over and above all other disciplines but that we should see all knowledge as fading, ephemeral, and nonbinding, that we should give ourselves over to a state of nonjudgment in a spiritual act of cognitive suspension. Of course, as the positive philosophers such as Plotinus noted, this idea already presumes a judgment for the truth of cognitive suspension and is self-refuting. Not much has changed.

On a more positive note, if you want to compare someone from the West with the Buddha, stop doing it with Meister Eckhart and Jesus and take up good ol' Sextus.

3. Jan/Feb 2016, 26.

4. Ibid., 78. Italics added.

5. Look, we Catholic intellectuals actually still read Aristotle. We don't take his science too seriously, even though we can contextualize his observations as "just fine for their time." But his understanding of what a cause means has influenced Catholic thought for centuries. Aristotle has four of them: the material, formal, efficient, and final causes of a thing. Contemporary intellectuals outside the Catholic framework, especially in the sciences, have lost sight of the formal and final causes of things. They merely focus on the material and efficient causes, which makes sense in the limitation the sciences call for. It doesn't make sense, after all, to ask what the purpose of a particular bacterium is and why God made it when our goal is to find a way to kill it without killing its host. But to think that knowledge ends with efficient and material causes is to cut oneself off from the most important types of knowledge, knowledge that, granted, doesn't save lives but makes lives worth living.

Chapter 8

1. Peter Balakian, *Black Dog of Fate: A Memoir* (New York: Broadway Books, 1997), 167.

2. Ibid., 168. A very simplistic idea has emerged in contemporary progressivism that Christians have always persecuted and never been persecuted. It's a silly idea, built on the real and true knowledge of American Christians' persecution of peoples, justifying black slavery, and promoting native genocide. The view is extremely, shall I say, American-centric, showing a lack of

knowledge for world histories. In the Armenian genocide, some of the main targets were Christians.

3. David E. Stannard, *American Holocaust: The Conquest of the New World* (New York: Oxford University Press, 1992), 74.

4. Barry Ferst, conversation, May 19, 2016.

5. Iris Chang, *The Rape of Nanking: The Forgotten Holocaust of World War II* (New York: Penguin, 1998); see the unnumbered photographs between pages 146 and 147.

6. Robert L. Berger, "Nazi Science—The Dachau Hypothermia Experiments," *New England Journal of Medicine* 322 (May 17, 1990): 1435–40.

Chapter 9

1. Pope Benedict, *Introduction to Christianity* (San Francisco: Ignatius, 2004), 138.

2. Isaiah 11:1.

3. I know. Everyone likes to say Jesus was subversive today, and it has become almost cliché in some circles and is even being critiqued. But denying Jesus's subversiveness would make for a very hipster move: arbitrarily denying a truth for a falsehood, choosing the worse things for better, like drinking a PBR over a good IPA or listening to Vampire Weekend over Paul Simon.

4. 1 Samuel 18:25, NRSV.

5. Matthew 21:14, NRSV.

6. Matthew 25:53, NRSV.

7. John 8:11, NRSV.

8. Matthew 8:18–22, NRSV.

9. Or at least as I interpret it as interpreting this relationship through a very defined set of glasses.

10. Also, don't think for one minute that my wife and I fulfill the beauty of such an ideal with any sense of achieved accomplishment. We're people and fail often, and our marriage only lives up to the love toward which it's called in the best of times. That's okay so long as the ideal remains because the ideal also produces mercy.

Conclusion

1. Pope Benedict, *Introduction to Christianity* (San Francisco: Ignatius, 2004), 143.

2. Augustine, *Confessions* (New York: Oxford University Press, 1998), Ch. X, 9.

3. Ibid., Ch. IV, 23.